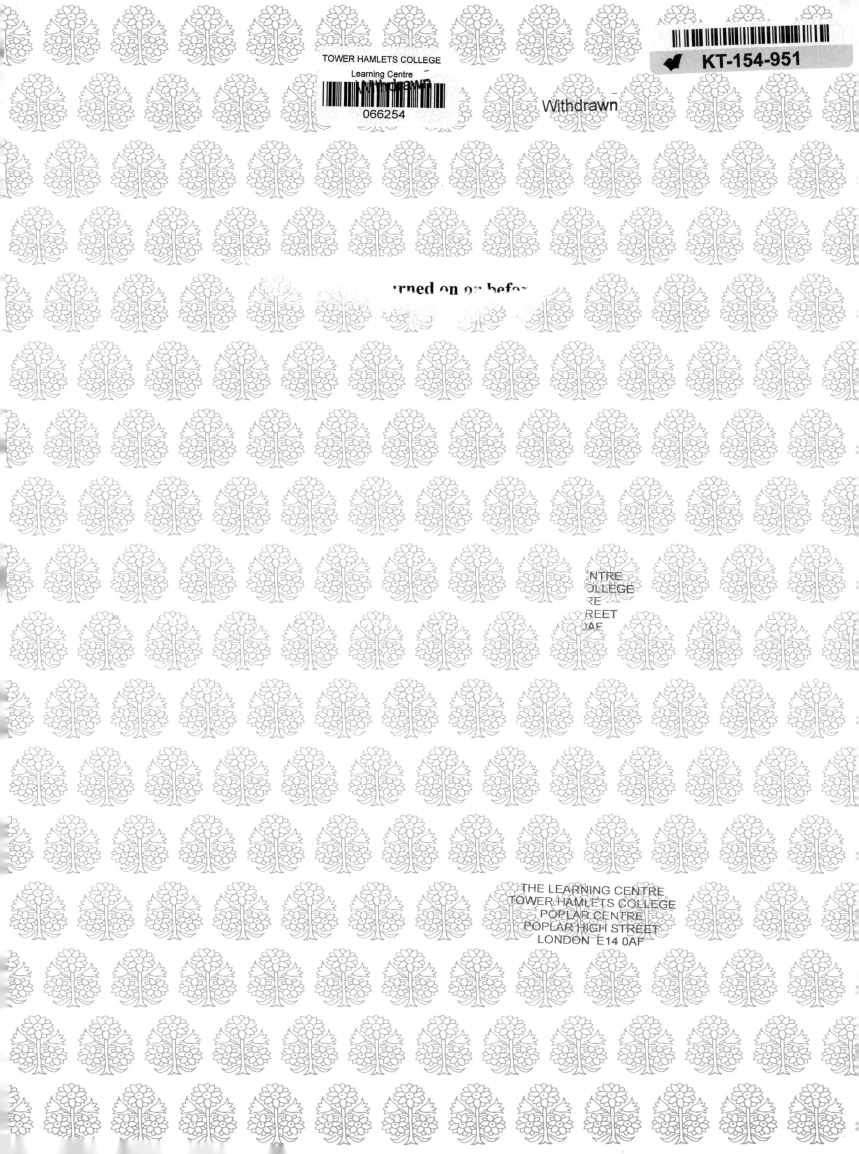

TOWER HAMLETS COLLEGE
Learning Centre
Withdrawn
066254

Withdrawn

KT-154-951

rned on or befor

NTRE
OLLEGE
RE
REET
0AF

THE LEARNING CENTRE
TOWER HAMLETS COLLEGE
POPLAR CENTRE
POPLAR HIGH STREET
LONDON E14 0AF

HINDUISM

Order No:

Class. 294 . 5 RAT.

Accession No: 066 254.

Type: L

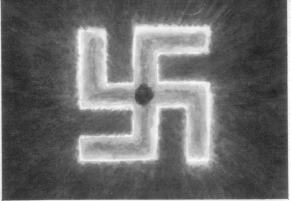

All rights reserved. No part of this publication may be transmitted or reproduced in any form or by any means without prior permission of the publisher.

ISBN: 1-85605-555-8

Text: Pramesh Ratnakar
Text Editor: Bela Butalia

Published in 2000 by **Silverdale Books**
An imprint of **Bookmart Ltd**
Registered Number 2372865
Trading as Bookmart Limited
Desford Road, Enderby
Leicester, LE9 5AD

© **Lustre Press Pvt. Ltd., 1996**
M 75 GK Part II (Market)
New Delhi 110 048, INDIA

Conceived and designed by Pramod Kapoor
at Roli CAD Centre

Photographs:
Ashok Khanna, Bindu Arora, Dheeraj Paul,
Gurmeet Thukral, Karoki Lewis, Krishna Dev,
P.K. Kapoor, Robyn Beeche, Roli Books Picture Library
Jacket photo: Avinash Pasricha

Illustrations:
A.Z. Ranjit, Sarat Mudli, Usha Subrahmanya,
K. Ramachandran

Printed and bound at
Star Standard Industries Pte. Ltd., Singapore

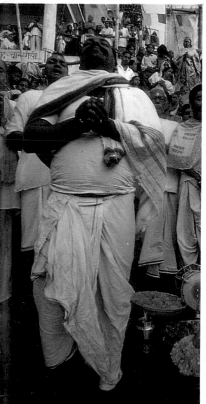

HINDUISM

Text
Pramesh Ratnakar

Silverdale Books

To brave little **Pooja Bhargava,**
To know you is to love you.

Son of Lord Shiva and Parvati, Ganesha, the elephant-headed deity, is widely worshipped as a god who brings good fortune and removes obstacles. Prayers are offered to him at the beginning of rituals, before leaving and entering houses or when faced with problems. His mount is the rat.

Contents

The character of the five Pandava brothers has been drawn with great delicacy and touch in the **Mahabharata**. *The poem illustrates certain high ideals associated with the concepts of* dharma *and virtues like brotherly love and truthfulness. Yudhisthira, the eldest of the Pandava brothers, is the son of the god Dharma and embodies the Hindu ideal of excellence. His name implies 'firm in battle'.*

Chapter 1

THE ESSENTIALS
OF HINDUISM

Once upon a time, the five Pandava brothers who had been forced into exile by their wily cousin Duryodhana were in search of water to quench their thirst. Yudhisthira, the eldest, sent his four younger brothers one by one into the wilderness in search of water. But when all four failed to return, he set out to search for them and by and by arrived at the edge of an enchanted pool. There he found all his brothers. They appeared to be dead. Grief-stricken, Yudhisthira, while approaching the water to quench his thirst, resolved to ascertain the cause of his brothers' death. But as he reached for the water, a voice rang out, 'Yudhisthira! I am the spirit of the lake. Do not touch the water. It belongs to me. If you do, you too will die like your brothers, who failed to heed my warning. However, if you are able to answer my questions, then you can drink from the pool.' Yudhisthira, the philosopher prince, agreed to answer the questions of the Spirit of the Lake. Yudhisthira's answers proved entirely satisfactory. Not only did he get to drink the water, but his brothers too were brought back to life.

The first question posed by the Spirit of the Lake to Yudhisthira and his answer sums up an essential of truth of Hinduism better than most learned discourses. The following questions and their answers provide in brief the essence of Hinduism and its world view.

Who makes the sun rise? What makes it shine?

Brahman makes the sun rise and it shines by the light of truth.

What kind of man can be considered the living dead, even though he breathes and is a respected and successful member of the community?

The man who does not really care for the gods, guests, elders of the family, ancestors and the divinity within—such a man can be considered to be the living dead.

What is heavier than earth? What is higher than the sky? What is faster than the wind? What is more numerous than straw?

A mother's pride and honour is heavier than the earth. The father is higher than the sky. Our desires fly faster than the wind and the things that we worry about are more numerous than straw.

Who is the friend of the traveller? Who is the friend of the householder? Who befriends an ill man? And who is the friend of the dead?

A fellow traveller is the friend of one who journeys. The wife is the friend of the man who stays at home. And it is the ability to give generously that eventually befriends the dead.

What should the true priest master? What makes him great? What limits him? What makes him evil?

The true priest is one who studies the Vedas in depth. Renunciation and ascetic practices make him great. Death limits him.

Criticizing and insulting others make him evil.

What limits a true warrior? What makes him evil?

Fear limits a true warrior. Not giving shelter and protection to the weak and the needy make him evil.

Who is the eternal host of all men? What is the nectar of immortality? What is Sanatana Dharma?

Fire is the eternal host of all human beings. Cow's milk is the nectar of immortality. And that which is everlasting and indestructible is Sanatana Dharma or Hinduism.

In this world what is the highest kind of action? What enables men to rise above sorrow? Friendship with which kind of a person never ends?

Mercy is the highest motive for action. Those who are in control of the five senses can rise above sorrow. And friendship with a wise and true man, who is not passion's slave, never ends.

What is it that man should reject to be loved by all? To be able to rise above sorrow? To be prosperous and happy?

He should reject egoistical pride to be loved by all. He should overcome anger to rise above sorrow. He should transcend desire to be truly prosperous. He should overcome greed to be happy.

What is it that covers the world? Why do men sacrifice friendship? What stops them from attaining heaven?

The world is covered with ignorance. Men sacrifice friendship because of greed. Inbred dissatisfactions stop men from attaining the bliss of heaven.

What is direction? What is water? What is food? What is poison?

The wise, true man is direction. Sky is water and the earth food. Desires are poison.

What is true wisdom? What is peace? What is the best form of kindness?

The apprehension of the ultimate divinity is wisdom. Stillness within is peace and to truly desire the happiness of all others is the best form of kindness.

Who is man's eternal enemy? Who is the true devotee of God? Who is the false devotee?

Anger is man's eternal enemy. One who desires the well being of all living creatures, he is the true devotee of God. The one who is cruel—he is the false devotee.

Who is truly happy? What is truly surprising? What is the true path?

The man who is not in debt and who lives ensconced amidst a caring family and community—he is truly happy. The fact that we see people dying all around us everyday and yet we live as if we will never die—that is truly surprising. There is no end to arguments and counter arguments, to visions and revisions. There is no single seer, however great he might be, whose words are not disputed, or whose words are meant to be the ultimate truth. The fact is that the ultimate truth is simply beyond. Therefore, the path which great and honoured men have often taken on their spiritual journeys—that is the true path.

The very name of Lord Rama is considered sacred. It is so charged with divinity that devotees often write out his name repeatedly in their quest for special merit. In ancient times Valmiki, an illiterate robber, attained supreme wisdom only by concentrating on the name of Rama. He went on to become a great poet saint who eventually composed the **Ramayana**.

A close-up of an ancient handwritten Sanskrit scripture.

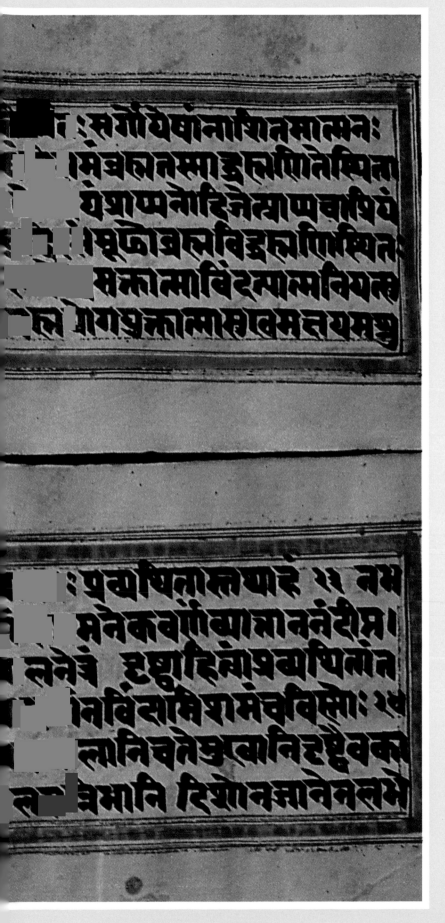

THE EVOLUTION OF HINDUISM

To understand Hinduism one has to begin with the Indus valley civilization, which is said to have flourished in the Indian subcontinent around 2700 BC. Since the script of the Indus valley people has not yet been deciphered, our knowledge of the religion and culture of this civilization must necessarily remain vague. However, extensive excavations in Harrappa and Mohenjo-daro and other Indus valley sites have yielded enough evidence to indicate that the worship of Shiva could possibly be traced to this source.

Once this is conceded, it is easy to assume that many traits of later Hinduism, specially those which cannot be directly traced to the Vedas, might have been a legacy of this civilization.

The presence of the great bath surrounded by small cells and of drained bathrooms in every house indicates that the Indus valley people stressed ritual purity through ablution. The fact that they did not bury but cremated their dead indicates some kind of belief in life after death. As for their gods, the evidence of the seals show that they probably practiced fertility cults; sites have yielded seals depicting mother goddesses representing the earth, the sacred bull (representing the sky), the peepal tree, and most significantly a horned ithyphallic god surrounded by animals—an elephant, a rhinoceros, a buffalo, a tiger, a long horned goat—and sitting in a yogic posture known as *utkatikasana*. The Indus valley god obviously bears remarkable resemblance to Lord Shiva—one of the great gods of later Hinduism.

No temple has been found so people most probably worshipped their gods at home—once again a very common Hindu practice to this day.

The Indus valley civilization appears to have reached a state of terminal decline by the time the Aryan migration into the subcontinent began in 1700 BC.

The Aryans who migrated into India obviously belonged to the same race whose descendants had migrated into Western Europe, for both shared the ancestral form of the Indo-European languages. Nomadic and warlike, the Aryan tribes entered India in waves spread over several centuries in the earlier half of the second millennium BC.

The Aryans brought with them horses, chariots and superior metallurgy. Though superior technologically, culturally the early Aryans seemed inferior to the Indus valley people. They did not have fixed settlements (let alone cities built in brick) nor did they seem to possess the art of reading, writing, or architecture.

The recorded textual history of the Hindus can be said to begin with the Vedas. The term does not denote any single book; it denotes an entire literature. The composition of the various texts which constitute the Vedas was spread over many centuries and over different localities, and is ascribed to many generations of poets and seers.

The Vedas constitute the Hindu revelation and it is traditionally claimed that no human agency was ever responsible for their creation. The Hindus believe that the Vedas have existed from the time of creation and will exist for all eternity. The various *rsis* or seers, it is believed, merely 'saw' or 'discovered' them with the help of their special intuitive insight. This has naturally given rise to another claim that the Vedas, free from all the limitations and deficiencies usually associated with the human agency, possess absolute validity.

From generation to generation the Vedas have been transmitted through the oral tradition. That is why the traditional term for the Vedas is *shruti* which means recited and heard, not written and read. Vedic literary history is usually divided into three periods: the Samhita, the Brahmana and the Upanishad period.

The Rig Veda, the earliest and the most important of the four Samhitas, is today recognized to be the world's oldest religious text. Composed between 1500 to 1000 BC, when the Aryans had settled down in the Punjab, the Rig Veda is a collection of 1,028 hymns divided into ten sections (or books).

Since the collected hymns were composed over centuries it is possible to deduce that the second to the seventh book are the oldest, while books eight, nine and ten come later.

The hymns are mostly addressed to a pantheon of gods who tended to lose their importance in later years. Some of the Rig Vedic gods are clearly pre-Vedic, having been worshipped from the most ancient days of Aryan history. These are Mitra the sun god, Varuna the god of the night or blue sky, Dyu and Prithvi the sky and earth gods, and Agni the fire god.

There are other deities which originated only in India, chief among them being Indra. Indra is easily the most important god in the Rig Veda and with his emergence Vedic mythology seems to have broken away from ancient Iranian practices and become distinguishable in its own right. The basic difference seems to lie in the way the later gods have been conceived. While the earlier gods were more magicians than gods, controlling the universe with their supernatural powers, the later gods are more warlike and heroic, performing supernatural feats in their eternal struggle against the demons to preserve the *rta*.

The future history of Hinduism was in fact rooted in the concept of *rta*. *Rta* refers to the cosmic order which in fact transcends the gods. The very role and function of the gods is determined in terms of this order. The gods try and preserve this order. On their part the demons are constantly trying to undermine it and this conflict serves as the basis of most of the Vedic myths.

The key Hindu concept of *dharma* is rooted in the concept of *rta*. *Dharma* as a concept unites all of Hinduism and links its different parts into a single totality. Derived from the Sanskrit root *dhr* (to bear, to support, to maintain) the word *dharma* literally means that which is established by law, duty, or custom.

Dharma is an order of values which links together the individual, the social and the cosmic on the basis of revelation contained in the Vedas. It is the structuring of reality in which it is possible to trace the consequences of each act, not merely in individual, social or ethical terms, but in cosmic terms. A *dharmic* act is one whose consequences are beneficial in terms of the entire cosmic process while an *adharmic* act endangers the whole universe.

In other words *dharma* offers to the world a vision of the Absolute, and then works out ways in which man can relate to it. It offers a vision of the cosmos, determines man's place in it and then sets about organizing the social and psychological world of its adherents in the light of the above. Insights relating to all three levels are offered as originating not so much from the human mind but as aspects of creation and therefore valid for all eternity. However, it is important not to think of *dharma* as a static concept. While concerned with the act and its consequences at all times, three stages can easily be marked out in the evolution of *dharma* as a concept. In the first stage the consequences of the ideal act were sought to be completely controlled by the power of the ritual; in the second stage the link between the ideal act and its consequences was sought to be broken by the power of mystical renunciation. And in the third stage the ideal act was seen as an occasion for surrender to a personal god in the fervour of devotion.

Hinduism has been shaped by what can be called its three main traditions: the ritualistic, the mystical and the devotional. Each of these are ways of visualizing the Absolute, relating to it and shaping the social world in the light of the Absolute. These three traditions have interacted with each other now for centuries. In different periods one or the other has emerged as dominant, but modern Hinduism is a rich synthesis of the three.

RITUAL TRADITION

The Hindu ritual tradition is rooted in the concept of the sacrifice as a cosmogenic act. From the earliest times the *yagna,* or fire sacrifice has been at the heart of the ritual. The very first hymn of the Rig Veda opens with an invocation to Agni, the god of fire. Underlying the fire sacrifice is the Rig Vedic understanding of Agni as a messenger carrying oblations to the world of gods.

When the Aryans first settled in the Punjab, the fire sacrifice was a simple affair—an offering of animals or foodgrains to the god of fire to propitiate the gods of wind, rain and thunder. But as contact with the indigenous populations increased, the sacrifice became increasingly elaborate and ritualistic, until only those who were especially trained could perform the complex rituals.

A new metaphysics was developed to reinforce the system. This metaphysics was elaborated in religious texts known as the Brahmanas, composed from about 700 BC onwards.

Brahmanas

The Brahmanas provide information on the religious life between the period of the Rig

Following pages 14-15: The havan *is a Vedic ritual of great antiquity and is an important part of Hindu religious ceremonies. During the* havan *offerings are made to Agni, the fire god, who is supposed to convey the wishes of the devotee to the Gods to the chanting of* mantras.

Veda and the Upanishads. Of the many Brahmanas, the most important are the Aitareya Brahmana and the Satapatha Brahmana. The Brahmanas are lengthy prose texts which describe, often in obscure symbolic terms, the major Vedic sacrifices.

The philosophy underlying these texts looks back to the Purusasukta myth of the Rig Veda, which describes the great sacrifice of the primeval man at the beginning of time and establishes sacrifice to be fundamental to the universal process. This famous hymn celebrates the creation of the world by the gods through the dismembering of the cosmic giant, Purusa or Prajapati, the primeval male person, who, in a typical Vedic paradox, is both the performer and the victim of the sacrifice. This sacrifice is believed to have created the whole universe. To maintain the universe in good working order constant repetitions of that original sacrifice were considered necessary as a re-enactment of the primeval sacrifice performed by the gods to create the universe, without which the cosmic order would disintegrate.

The implications of this theory and practice were to prove crucial for the future of Hinduism. This became the basis of the hierarchical vision of man. Madeleine Biardeau (*Hinduism: The Anthropology of a Civilization*) has rightly pointed out that the four castes or *varnas* are first and foremost defined in orthodox theory by a specific relation to this rite. The Brahmin is the priest who conducts the sacrifice; the Kshatriya (the warrior) is the 'sacrificing agent' and at the same time the possessor of the strength which protects the Brahmins and all other men; the Vaishya (the trader), in addition to his role as a 'sacrificing agent', is the producer of the wealth required for the maintenance of the ritual activity without which there can be no prosperity on earth.

As for the Shudras, they must serve the three higher *varnas*. Their relationship to the rite is indirect but not entirely absent. Yet it is distant enough to place them on the boundary of what is human, where there is nothing to hope for but a better rebirth.

Then there are those even lower in the social hierarchy. There is no *karma* conceivable for them; they have to live away from the high castes in a space which is neither human nor wild, at a level in the scale of beings lower than domestic animals. These are the untouchables.

Women are not regarded as having autonomous ritual activity, but they are necessarily associated with the rites performed by their husbands. Thus they have no personal destiny in life, and after death the most virtuous are rewarded by being reunited with their husbands. To be reborn as a woman, even in a Brahmin family, is therefore in orthodox theory another form of expiation of past sins.

The capacity to perform rituals was seen as the defining feature of humanity, and the Brahmins, who could sustain this ritual activity, came to be seen as being even more powerful than the gods: the verses or *mantras* themselves practically became the gods, and the effect of the sacrifice was not regarded as a gift from the gods, but was believed to follow automatically from the scrupulously punctilious performance of the different parts of the sacrifice and the proper pronunciation and accenting of the *mantras*. Obviously the people who performed the sacrifice, the priestly class of Brahmins, emerged as the dominant social group, for theoretically, through the power of the ritual they could force the gods to perform according to their will.

Rituals ranging from simple, daily domestic fire sacrifices to the year-long elaborate royal sacrifices like the Ashwamedha Yagna, involving the slaughter of thousands of animals, came to dominate existence. A vast corpus of texts was produced which laid down norms for the social and ritual behaviour of every Hindu.

The Srauta Sutras, dealing with sacrificial ritual, give instructions for the establishment of the three sacred fires of the sacrifice (*agnihotra*) as well as for other Vedic rituals. Connected with these was the Sulva Sutra, which gives exact rules for the measurement and construction of the sacred sacrificial ground and the fire altars.

The Grhya Sutras, dealing with domestic rituals and rites of passage, are manuals explaining the domestic (*grhya*) religious ceremonies. Along with descriptions of many popular customs, these texts contain ritual procedures for the performance of the *samskaras*, or Hindu sacraments. About forty in number, these ritual procedures cover the entire life of a person from the moment of conception of life to the hour of death and include funerary ceremonies and rites (*sraddha*) for the departed soul. The most important ones, centring around conception, the initiation of a child as a twice-born (*dvija*), education, marriage and death, are still performed by most pious Hindus.

The Dharma Sutras, which deal with morals, ethics, law and politics, are manuals explaining proper human conduct. They cover a wide range of subjects encompassing religious matters—including rules for worship, purification and expiatory rites, use of food as well as lectures on cosmology, cosmogony, eschatology and sections on civil, criminal and family law. They also establish the four *ashrams* (stages of life) for the first time, along with rules for the proper behaviour of members of the Aryan community.

During the early centuries of the common era, the Sutras were expanded into Dharam Shastras, text books on the sacred and secular duty of all members of the Aryan community, which offered a model of a perfectly ordered society, and were also used in courts of law. The *Manu Smriti* was an early but most influential text of this category. *Yajnavalkaya Smriti* stands next to *Manu* in prestige, but is a more modern, advanced and clearer presentation.

Practically every aspect of the ideal life of Hindu men and women is addressed in these texts, leaving no doubt as to the proper course of conduct in a given situation. These texts were worked over in successive periods, but the essentials go back to around 500 BC. They were the sole domain of learned Brahmins who established and changed the precepts as and when the need arose. An essential feature of this comprehensively mapped out social and individual existence was the fact that society must at all times recognize the superiority of the Brahmin, give him his due respect and look after him economically so that he could devote himself to his holy work.

MYSTICAL TRADITION

The very success of the rituals helped to foster reaction. In time it came to be believed that the accumulated power of the rituals could not possibly be used up in one lifetime—that power might well wash over the temporary boundary of death into new birth and life.

For the Rig Vedic Aryan, death meant a crossing over to the world of ancestors. Hence, it was the duty of the living to perform propitiatory rites for the ancestors, while the latter in their turn looked after the interests of their family members. But as the significance of the rituals increased it came to be argued that the power of rituals performed during the lifetime would continue to benefit the individual directly even after death.

Once the boundary between the life now and the life after death had been dissolved, the idea of rebirth, where actions done in this life would continue to affect the course of events in the next, became acceptable. One comes across the doctrine of rebirth for the first time in the Chandogya Upanishad, in which it is asserted that the birth of a child takes place as a result of a series of sacrifices performed by the gods. In heaven the gods offer faith and produce Soma (moon). In mid-space they offer Soma and produce rain clouds. On earth they offer rain and produce food. In man they offer food and produce semen. In women they offer semen and a child is produced. After a man's death, he is burnt on the funeral pyre and his soul, if he has done good deeds in life, passes to the world of ancestors. But once his stock of merit is exhausted, he passes on to the moon, from there into space, from space to the wind, from the wind to the rain, and from the rain it comes back to earth and turns into food, from food it turns to semen and from semen to rebirth. And so the cycle goes on over and over again.

In the long run it turned out to be the very idea of rebirth which undermined Brahminical ritualism, for the constant cycle of birth, death and rebirth came to be seen as infinitely wearying—and release from the cycle, or *moksha,* became the highest possible goal for a Hindu.

Though orthodox Brahminism kept insisting on the need for ritual acts, it came to be seen that action, especially ritual action, condemned man to endless rebirth and death. The only escape from this perpetual flux—*samsara*—was by removing oneself from the mechanism of *karma,* and therefore, from human society, by an explicit renunciation of all that one had been till that time:

> But unsafe are the boats of sacrifice to go to the farthest shore . . . imagining religious ritual and gifts of charity as the final good, the unwise see not the path supreme. Indeed they have in high heaven the reward of their pious action; but thence they fall to earth or even down to lower regions . . . but those who in purity and faith live in solitude of the forest . . . those in radiant purity pass through the gates of the sun to the dwelling place supreme where the Spirit is in eternity.
> Beholding the worlds of creation, let the lover of God attain renunciation: what is above creation cannot be attained by action. In his longing for divine wisdom, let him go with reverence to a teacher, in whom live the sacred words and whose whole soul has peace in Brahman.
>
> (MUNDAKA UPANISHAD)

Upanishads

Composed from the 6th century BC onwards the Upanishads develop the mystical and metaphysical dimension of Hinduism. Widely known and widely quoted, the key ideas of the Upanishads have become a part of the spiritual make-up of the average Hindu.

The word 'upanishad' literally means 'sitting near'. The Upanishads are speculative treatises, with most of them depicting legendary sages or gods imparting wisdom to their disciples. Tradition lists 108 Upanishads. However of these only 13 are considered genuine appendices of the Vedas and the Brahmanas. The earlier Upanishads are in prose. The later ones are in verse or mixed prose and verse.

At the heart of the Upanishads' vision is the profound consciousness of the indivisible wholeness of life. The texts were inspired by the vision of God in all things and all things in God.

According to the Upanishads there exists a cosmic spirit—infinite, creative, benevolent, deathless. It pervades everything. It is the final, transcendent truth—the one cause for which there is no cause, the real power behind all tangible forces, the consciousness which animates all conscious beings. It is a vast ageless ocean of which everything that is experienced is only a wave.

The Upanishads often tend to characterize the ultimate Spirit as being *nirguna,* that is, 'without attributes', and describe it in the neutral gender as an impersonal essence that cannot be named or described because it transcends all categories:

> Who sends the mind to wander afar? Who first drives life to start on its journey? Who impels us to utter these words? Who is the spirit behind the eye and the ear?
> It is the ear of the ear, the eye of the eye, and the word of words, the mind of mind, and the life of life . . .
> There the eye goes not, nor words, nor mind. We know not, we cannot understand, how he can be explained. He is above the known and he is above the unknown . . .
>
> (KENA UPANISHAD)

In the Upanishads the term generally used to describe this cosmic spirit is either Purusa or Brahman and it is said to exist on two levels simultaneously. On one level it is the ultimate truth of the universe, but on another level it exists within us as *atman*—our own inner subjective truth. It is the heart of all hearts, the core of all cores—the immanent aspect of the transcendent Brahman:

> There is a Spirit that is mind and life, light and truth and vast spaces. He contains all works and desires and all perfumes and all tastes. He enfolds the whole universe, and in silence is loving to all.
> This is the spirit that is in my heart, smaller than the grain of rice, or a grain of canary seed, or the kernel of a grain of canary seed. This is the spirit that is in my heart, greater than the earth, greater than the sky, greater than the heaven itself, greater than all these worlds.
> He contains all works and desires and all perfumes and all tastes. He enfolds the whole universe and in silence is loving to all. This is the spirit that is in my heart, this is Brahman.
>
> (CHANDOGYA UPANISHAD)

Atman is different from both the personality and the self, for it is nothing less than the eternal within us, a constant amidst all the changes and activities of the universe. The identity of Brahman and *atman* is summed up in the famous formula, *'Tat Tvam As'* (thou art that).

> 'Bring me the fruit from this Banyan tree.'
> 'Here it is, father.'
> 'Break it.'
> 'It is broken, Sir.'
> 'Break one of them, my son.'
> 'It is broken, Sir.'
> 'What do you see in it?'
> 'Nothing at all, Sir.'
> Then his father spoke to him: 'My son, from the very essence in the seed which you cannot see comes in truth this vast Banyan tree. Believe me, my son, an invisible and subtle essence is the Spirit of the whole universe. That is reality. That is the *atman*. THOU ART THAT.'

Discovering the identity of Brahman and *atman* within ourselves, argue the Upanishads, is the ultimate goal of human existence. The seeker must specially train himself to enable the *atman* to realize its full identity with Brahman. The realization will ensure that the *atman* is not born again and again, but will enjoy the intense bliss of Brahman forever.

The Upanishads transform the ideas and symbols contained in the Vedas and the Brahmanas. For example, in the sacrificial tradition the pride of place was given to horse sacrifice. The Upanishads in a characteristic strategic twist do not speak of a flesh and blood horse but of one whose 'head is the Dawn, whose eyes are the Sun and whose mane is Heaven itself'. Instead of the ordinary sacrificial fire, they talk of the fire of meditation. Their aim always is to encourage the aspirant to withdraw the mind's eye from external things and direct it inwards.

This is the Jnana Marga (the Way of Knowledge) to liberation. The knowledge in question, however, is not intellectual knowledge, but rather deep, intuitive self-awareness triggered by intense, disciplined meditation under the guidance of the guru.

Buddhism

The challenge of mysticism contained in the Upanishads was pushed to its logical conclusion by Buddhism. Both Buddhism and the Upanishads emphasize that there is no release from rebirth either by the performance of sacrifice or practice of severe penance. It is the perception of truth, the knowledge of reality which is the basis of all existence and which can liberate the soul. The feeling that this life is suffering and the life hereafter is that which we long for, is accepted by both. The vital teachings of the Upanishads, the oneness of all life, were also accepted by Buddha.

Unlike the Upanishads though Buddhism formally rejected both the caste system as well as the authority of the Brahmins. The Buddha emphasized natural law over supernaturalism. Each man could gain salvation for himself without the mediation of a priest or without reference to the gods. The world of experience, according to the Buddha, does not require any god for its explanation. The causality of the law of *karma* will do. Buddha tried to shift the focus from the worship of god to the service of man and started a religion independent of dogma and priesthood, sacrifice and sacrament.

Buddha's insistence on *ahimsa*—the absence of the desire to kill—directly undermined Vedic sacrifices as the latter included animal slaughter. This led to the undermining of the orthodox Brahminical world order as well. So much so, in course of time the Brahmins introduced coconuts in place of animals as the symbolic objects of sacrifice during the performance of rituals and they themselves emerged as the most vehement proponents of vegetarianism, thereby occupying and controlling once again the higher moral ground. In modern times when Mahatma Gandhi challenged British imperialism as well as the traditional caste system, he made *ahimsa* the cornerstone of his political and ethical philosophy.

CLASSICAL SCHOOLS OF PHILOSOPHY

The rise of Buddhism, Jainism and other heterodox sects forced the Hindus to formulate their doctrines in a more coordinated and logical form. This led to the formulation of the six classical schools of philosophy, linked in three pairs: Nyaya and Vaisheshika; Karman and Uttara Mimamsa; Samkhya and Yoga.

The **Nyaya and Vaisheshika** schools emphasize reason and analysis. They are grounded in logic and seek to critically examine accepted notions of traditional philosophy through the canons of logical proof. Kashyap's *Vaisheshika Nyaya Sutra* and Gautam's *Nyaya Sutra* are the main texts of this school.

The school of **Purva Mimamsa** ('Former Investigation') sometimes called **Karman Mimamsa** ('Ritual Investigation') deals with the sacrificial part of the Vedas, while the **Uttara Mimamsa** ('Later Investigation'), also known as Vedanta ('End of the Vedas'), deals with the Upanishads, and is by far the best known branch of Indian philosophy.

The basic tenets of the philosophy of **Samkhya** are now a part of the overall structure of Hinduism and so need to be examined in some detail. Samkhya recognizes three kinds of evidence: perception, inference and *shruti* (Vedic revelation). It divides the universe into spirit (*purusa*) and nature (*prakriti*). The latter is further subdivided into three constituent qualities or *gunas*: goodness (*sattva*), energy (*rajas*) and darkness (*tamas*).

Samkhya philosophy states that the original creative principle is not one but two: *purusa* and *prakriti*. The *purusa* or the Absolute, is beyond all qualities and classifications. Logically it cannot even be said that it exists or that it does not exist. Yet it is the source from which everything originates, to which everything returns. It is pure consciousness and as it is without attributes it cannot convert itself into the world of phenomena.

Like *purusa*, *prakriti* too is timeless, permanent but unlike the former it is capable of creation and action. It is the feminine principle. It is pure energy. The created universe then is an aspect of *prakriti*. But like *prakriti* itself it exists only for the *purusa*, though it does not owe its existence and activity to the latter.

Facing page: Buddha broke away from the rigid Brahminism prevalent in his times, rejecting the Vedas, the caste system and even the Hindu concept of liberation. But the Hindus, instead of treating him as an adversary, incorporated him within their religious fold by transforming him into the ninth incarnation of Vishnu.

Prakriti has two opposing phases, both operating continuously and simultaneously. The first one integrates. This is *sristi* or the creative phase. The second one is the reverse process, *laya* or *samhara* (dissolution, by which the manifested universe returns to its original unmanifested state). These two processes are ever-present in nature; what our senses recognize as the universe of phenomenon is simply the result of these two processes. The quality underlying the integrative or creative process is known as *rajoguna*; the quality underlying the disintegrating or *laya* process is termed *tamoguna*; and the quality attached to the phenomenal phase of nature, that is, serving phenomenal existence is *sattvaguna*.

These properties do not belong to *purusa*, but only to *prakriti*. These gunas of *prakriti* are also to be seen in man, who is part of *prakriti*. In man the qualities that help to preserve the universe as a whole are regarded as *sattvaguna*; those that help to create affection are *rajoguna* and those that tend to bring about disintegration are known as *tamoguna*.

Nothing in the realm of *prakriti* will be free of these three *gunas*: what one meets will always be a complex of all three, with one or the other aspect dominating.

Prakriti or nature is subdivided into two parts: the *para* and the *apara*. The former denotes the intangible world of spirituality with the three subtle elements, *manas* (mind, or the faculty of perception), *buddhi* (intellect, or the faculty of reasoning), and *ahankara* (egoism or the sense). The latter denotes the tangible material world made up of the five gross elements or *panchbhuta* (earth, water, fire, air and ether).

The ultimate aim of Samkhya is to dissolve the apparent dualism between *prakriti* and *purusa*, and unite them through *gyan* or consciousness.

Yoga is very closely related to Samkhya and adds the element of the Lord *(Ishvara)* and a method of attaining the ultimate goal by mastering body and mind through physical exercises and meditation.

Yoga maintains that since Brahman in one or the other form is located within us, he could be perceived by self-realization, which is possible only if we withdraw our senses from the external world and discover the reality within. In the *Yoga Sutra*, Patanjali describes the process of physical and mental discipline that could lead a disciple to this self-realization. The discipline is known as Raj Yoga or Astanga Yoga. It involves:

1. *Yama* (mental control): The yogi to begin with must cultivate non-violence, truth, non-theft, celibacy, continence and non-acquisitiveness.
2. *Niyam* (spiritual observances): This involves deep insightful study of sacred texts, contemplation of God, practice of austerities, contentment and devotion to God.
3. *Asana* (posture): This involves cultivating the ability to adopt a suitable posture while meditating. The idea is that the physical body should serve as an aid to meditation rather than an impediment. The posture should help eliminate disturbances or distractions.
4. *Pranyama* (breath control): The deliberate control of the body's respiratory activity is possible only with the help of a trained teacher. Breath control is actually an exercise in controlling *manas*, the life force which energizes the different organs of the body.
5. *Pratyahar* (withdrawal of the mind from the world of senses): This step involves developing the skill to separate the mind from the sensory inputs that bombard it all the time. Here the yogi seeks to control disturbances from external sources. This requires a major psychological effort as well for it is possible only by developing a certain attitude of detachment to the external world.
6. *Dharana* (concentration): In this stage the yogi is able to keep his mind steadily focused on a single thought, *mantra* or on some part of the body

like the middle of the eyebrows or the heart.

7. *Dhyana* (deep contemplation): The mind now slips into another dimension of reality and the world of phenomena falls away.

8. *Samadhi* (trance or total absorption): This is the final stage when the withdrawal from the external world is complete and one realizes the splendour of the *atman* within. Yogic self-realization is considered to be impossible without the guidance of an enlightened teacher.

All the philosophic schools had a similar pattern of development. The philosophic views of a great sage in the dim past were elaborated and defended from the criticism of the opponents by successive generations of thinkers. This led to the gradual systematization of the philosophical views. Jamini's *Purva Mimamsa* is the most important text for the ritualistic Mimamsa school while the *Brahma Sutras* attributed to Badrayana are the basic texts of the Vedanta. The basic concepts of the philosophy of Samkhya are elucidated in the *Sankyakarika* of Ishvara Krishna. The *Yoga Sutra* of Patanjali constitutes the basic text of the yoga school.

DEVOTIONAL TRADITION: BHAKTI

Around the second century BC a major development took place which triggered the emergence of the Hindu tradition as we know it today. The notion that came to the fore was that of *bhakti* or ecstatic devotion to a personal god.

Bhakti involved an entirely new view of the Absolute and an entirely new way of realizing it. Its beginnings are to be found in the Svetasvatra and Kena Upanishads where the impersonal Absolute is transformed into a personal deity by being given a name and a personality. In the Svetasvatra Upanishad this personal deity is called Shiva and in the Kena Upanishad it is called Vishnu. However, the single-most important text that firmly established *bhakti* as the dominant Hindu mode of relating to the gods was the *Bhagvad Gita*. Scholars have pointed out that the ritual and mystical traditions of Hinduism are rooted in values and ideas structurally opposed to each other. The ritual tradition points to the involvement with the world and its orderly organization in hierarchical terms. The mystical tradition points towards renunciation of the world and emphasizes universalism and monism. Ultimately it is the tension that obtained between the two that shaped Hinduism.

Bhagvad Gita

At the time of composition of the *Bhagvad Gita* sometime around 250 BC these two sets of opposed ideas and philosophies confronted each other, as might two armies in the battlefield for the right to rule over the Hindu mind of future generations. It is in terms of the opposition between the two polarities in values that Arjuna's doubts and Krishna's intervention in the *Bhagvad Gita* assume significance. It is Lord Krishna in the *Bhagvad Gita* who resolves the structural opposition between the two polarities, giving rise to new speculations and new practices in which these two irreconcilable principles come to coexist.

It is because the *Bhagvad Gita* resolves not just the doubts of an Arjuna on the eve of the battle of Mahabharata, but also the essential ideological conflict of Hinduism that it has come to occupy a unique place in Hindu sacred literature. Today it is a pan-Hindu text, its authority and influence transcending sectarian as well as regional considerations.

The context in which Krishna delivers his message is intensely dramatic. As the two great armies of the cousins, the Pandavas and the Kauravas, face each other in Kurukshetra, Arjuna suddenly loses the will to act. On the one hand he realizes that his duty as a Kshatriya prince is to fight in righteous warfare. On the other he sees that he must necessarily kill his own friends, relatives and teachers. He feels like giving it all up—the claims of the kingdom, the desire for revenge, action itself.

Caught between the claims of the *dharma* of his caste and the seductive pull of renunciation, he turns to Krishna for advice. Krishna is Arjuna's charioteer and the image of the charioteer expresses the function of spiritual guide performed by the human form of the supreme God in this battle of *dharma*. His is a new message in Hindu theology, the message of an affectionate personal God, delivered directly to the devotee. It preserves the essential framework of orthodox Brahminism and yet revolutionizes it from within.

Krishna begins with traditional logic which is grounded in the acceptance of social hierarchy. He repeatedly asserts that it is better to perform one's own duty, however badly, than to perform well that of another.

He tells Arjuna that he has to follow his Kshatriya *dharma,* failing which he would be the object of scorn of all his peers and would be thrown into hell after his death.

But he then puts forward the remarkable new proposition, which is the essential message of the *Gita*—the doctrine of motiveless action. One should observe one's *dharma* with complete disregard for the consequences. One should act without thinking about personal gain or loss, for thoughts about the fruits of the world will prevent the integration of the self and the achievement of the ultimate spiritual goal. Krishna argues that only this 'disinterestedness' can enable a human being to achieve the ultimate ideal of escaping from the 'bondage of the act'. 'Set thy heart upon thy work, but never on its reward. Work not for a reward, but never cease to do thy work' (*Bhagvad Gita* 2:47).

For Krishna, avoiders of action, or those who are followers of renunciation philosophies are as misguided as the Vedic ritualists, for he asserts that no one ever ceases to act even for an instant; therefore a man must perform the set acts given by creation but he who is aware of the reality of the *atman* within performs his duties without a thought for rewards: 'Not by refraining from action does man attain freedom from action. Not by mere

renunciation does he attain supreme perfection . . . the world is in bonds of action, unless the action is consecration. Let thy actions then be pure, free from the bonds of desire' (Ibid. 3:56).

Finally, Krishna puts forward the second important new proposition. He argues that the disinterestedness he is advocating is possible only through an unconditional surrender of the self to a God from whom all things and all beings have emanated and through whom they subsist and perish. The purity of the motive itself is to be ensured not by vigilance, introspection, analysis and watchfulness, but by the surrender of the ego in a fervour of devotion, to a personal deity who is nevertheless responsible for everything in the world: 'Know thou that whatever is beautiful and good, whatever has glory and power is only a portion of my own radiance . . . But of what help is it to thee to know this diversity? Know that with one single fraction of my Being I pervade and support the Universe, and know that I AM' (Ibid. 10:41-2).

This all-embracing aspect of the divine is the theme of the famous theophany of the eleventh chapter, where Krishna displays himself to Arjuna in all the glory of his celestial form, with 'the brilliance of a thousand suns'.

Krishna goes on to suggest that it is *bhakti*, or love and devotion, which is the bond of union between man and the supreme deity. 'He who in the oneness of love, loves me in whatever he sees, wherever this man may live, in truth this man lives in me' (Ibid. 6:31). The *Gita* says again and again that *bhakti* is the way to reach God: 'By love he knows me in truth, who I am and what I am' (Ibid. 18:55). 'Only by love can men see me, and know me and come unto me' (Ibid. 11:54).

The notion of *bhakti* is perhaps the most important new teaching of the *Gita* and the doctrine of motiveless action is linked to it. Whatever a person does should be done not for himself but for the love and glory of the ever-present God, for then he ceases to be in a real sense an actor but becomes a means of action, merely fulfilling God's work. If through *bhakti* one can remove one's own ego and one's desires as motives for action, then whatever one might do, it is in fact God himself who is acting through you. 'For concentration is better than mere practice, and meditation is better than concentration; but higher than meditation is surrender in love of the fruit of one's actions, for on surrender follows peace' (Ibid. 12:12).

The concept of *avtara* or incarnation reinforces this doctrine of *bhakti*. Krishna

Thus we are told that even if a very evil man devotes himself to Krishna alone, his soul will quickly become righteous, and he will go to eternal rest.

The later career of Hinduism was shaped by the *bhakti* philosophy. New gods, with wider, more universal appeal appeared as the focal point of this new type of religiosity. As they rose to prominence they incorporated various other local deities (*yakshas, nagas, ganas*) as well as the Vedic deities of earlier times in their entourage.

Krishna in playful dalliance with Radha who is his eternal consort. The symbolism enjoined in the exclusive relationship with Radha, the chief among the many beloved gopis, *is that worldly life offers no bar to salvation, and the highest spiritual objective is to join in the eternal sport of Radha-Krishna.*

appears to be a normal human being yet he is also the Lord of all Beings, that is, Vishnu, who through his supernatural power has taken on a human form for the protection of the good, the destruction of evil and the establishment of righteousness *(dharma).*

An important consequence of this new religious approach in which the great God can intervene directly in human affairs is the slackening of the iron law of *karma*. To the perfect *bhakta* (devotee), Krishna's grace can overcome all other factors including the law of *karma*, and can in a moment transform his life and set him on the path to true liberation.

The village *devis* came to be seen as facets of the great goddess. The concept of *avtara* allowed Hinduism to incorporate in its fold all the popular local deities as manifestations or incarnations of supreme gods. By the 8th century AD even Buddha was being considered an incarnation of Vishnu. The Hindu pantheon ended up containing 330 million gods, though two gods, Vishnu and Shiva, now reign supreme. The introduction of idol worship ensured that statues and symbols of gods were housed in impressive temples all over India which the devotee could worship with offerings of flowers, foodgrain, water and milk.

The Gita and Gandhi

*The entire **Bhagwad Gita** revolves around the cruel predicament faced by Arjuna on the eve of battle: whether to wage war against his kinsmen or not? Krishna, who is Arjuna's charioteer, not only resolves the latter's doubts but also instructs him in the meaning of existence.*

The *Bhagvad Gita* was Gandhi's 'spiritual dictionary', the 'mother' who never let him down. Recitations from the *Gita* were a regular feature at his *ashrams* (retreats). His letters abound with references to the *Gita* which he translated into Gujarati. In two published books he has presented a detailed interpretation of his favourite scripture. For Gandhi the essence of the *Gita* was expressed in the last twenty stanzas of chapter 2 (stanzas 54-72). He repeatedly asserted that with chapter 2 the *Gita* ended, and that it did not need to be followed by anything more, as the rest of the text was a mere elaboration of the basic message contained in the last verses of chapter two.

In the *Gita*, Lord Krishna, an incarnation of the great god Vishnu, persuades Arjuna to take up arms in the war against the Kauravas. But for Gandhi, the *Gita* neither promotes violence, nor is it about devotion or *bhakti* to a personal deity. It is an allegorical work in which the poet has seized upon the occasion of the war between the Pandavas and the Kauravas to draw attention to the conflict within ourselves between the forces of good and evil.

For Gandhi the fundamental aim of a great religion is not to promote blind devotionalism, but self-realization by controlling the senses, the mind and the ego, and ethical action here and now.

Gandhi's favourite lines are Krishna's answer to Arjuna's specific request for a description of the person who has achieved perfect control over his inner self, over feelings of love, lust and attachment, and who has reached a state of perfect equanimity to all that may please or displease him.

Bhagavad Gita

(Chapter II: Stanzas 54-72)

THE CHARACTERISTICS OF THE PERFECT SAGE

Arjuna said:

(54) What is the description of the man who has this firmly founded wisdom, whose being is steadfast in spirit, O Kesava (Krsna)? How should the man of settled intelligence speak, how should he sit, how should he walk?

The Blessed Lord said:

(55) When a man puts away all the desires of his mind, O Partha (Arjuna), and when his spirit is content in itself, then is he called stable in intelligence.

(56) He whose mind is untroubled in the midst of sorrows and is free from eager desire amid pleasures, he from whom passion, fear, and rage have passed away, he is called a sage of settled intelligence.

(57) He who is without affection on any side, who does not rejoice or loathe as he obtains good or evil, his intelligence is firmly set (in wisdom).

(58) He who draws away the senses from the objects of sense on every side as a tortoise draws in his limbs (into the shell), his intelligence is firmly set (in wisdom).

(59) The objects of sense turn away from the embodied soul who abstains from feeding on them but the taste for them remains. Even the taste turns away when the Supreme is seen.

(60) Even though a man may ever strive (for perfection) and be ever so discerning, O Son of Kunti (Arjuna), his impetuous senses will carry off his mind by force.

(61) Having brought all (the senses) under control, he should remain firm in yoga intent on Me; for he, whose senses are under control, his intelligence is firmly set.

(62) When a man dwells in his mind on the objects of sense, attachment to them is produced. From attachment springs desire and from desire comes anger.

(63) From anger arises bewilderment, from bewilderment loss of memory; and from loss of memory, the destruction of intelligence and from the destruction of intelligence he perishes.

(64) But a man of disciplined mind, who moves among the objects of sense, with the senses under control and free from attachment and aversion, he attains purity of spirit.

(65) And in that purity of spirit, there is produced for him an end of all sorrow; the intelligence of such a man of pure spirit is soon established (in the peace of the self).

(66) For the uncontrolled, there is no intelligence; nor for the uncontrolled is there the power of concentration and for him without concentration, there is no peace and for the unpeaceful, how can there be happiness?

(67) When the mind runs after the roving senses, it carries away the understanding, even as a wind carries away a ship on the waters.

(68) Therefore, O Mighty-armed (Arjuna), he whose senses are all withdrawn from their objects his intelligence is firmly set.

(69) What is night for all beings is the time of waking for the disciplined soul; and what is the time of waking for all beings is night for the sage who sees (or the sage of vision).

(70) He unto whom all desires enter as waters into the sea, which, though ever being filled is ever motionless, attains to peace and not he who hugs his desires.

(71) He who abandons all desires and acts free from longing, without any sense of mineness or egotism, he attains to peace.

(72) This is the divine state (brahmisthiti) O Partha (Arjuna), having attained thereto, one is (not again) bewildered; fixed in that state even at the end (at the hour of death) one can attain to the bliss of God (brahmanirvana).

Krishna

Born in the prison of the evil king Kansa, who wanted to have him killed, Krishna was miraculously saved and smuggled to Gokula, where he was brought up in a community of cowherds. The Bhagavata Purana delights in giving details of the divine Krishna's mischievous pranks as a boy and his amorous pursuit of the *gopis*. The Krishna of this period is often represented as a handsome youth with flowing hair and a flute in his hands.

Krishna appears prominently in the *Mahabharata* but it is in the Puranas, especially the Bhagvat Purana that the story of his life is told in great detail.

In the epic *Mahabharata,* Krishna is shown to be directly related to the Pandava brothers through his aunt Kunti who is their mother. Throughout the epic he acts as a philosopher, guide and friend to the Pandavas.

He is present at the *svyamavar* of Draupadi, where he declares that she was fairly won by Arjuna. He helps Arjuna to find a spouse for his sister, Subhadra. Together with the Pandavas, he attacks and kills Jarasanda, king of Magadha, who had forced him to leave Mathura and emigrate to Dwarka.

At the Rajasuya Yagna, performed by Yudhisthira, Krishna slays Sisu-pala who was intent on disrupting the holy proceedings. After the famous gambling match between Yudhisthira and Shakuni, it is Krishna who saves Draupadi from being disrobed.

Before the actual war starts, Krishna, as the messenger of the Pandavas, delivers a powerful message of peace to the Kaurava court and later in the course of the war, though he does not take up arms himself, acts as Arjuna's charioteer, helping the Pandavas on innumerable occasions. In fact, it is Krishna's presence which constitutes the difference between the two armies and but for his guidance

it can be fairly said that the Pandavas would never have won the war.

At the end of the war it is he who saves the last surviving heir of the Pandavas from the destructive weapon of Ashavasthama. After the war he returns to Dwarka, but there one day all the Yadav chieftains get slaughtered in a drunken brawl. Krishna himself gets killed while asleep, by a hunter named Jaras who mistakes him for a deer.

Krishna, the great god with universal appeal who reveals himself to Arjuna in the **Bhagavad Gita** *as the Supreme God, is also the pastoral cowherd deity whose playful childhood and romantic youth are celebrated in Braj (Vrindavan), his homeland. Krishna's youthful dalliance with his beloved milkmaid companions (gopis) or* kanta-bhaktas *is a symbol of divine love developed to its fullest degree, to the state of* mahabhava *or supreme love. Krishna plays the flute to attract the gopis. His* ras *(relish)* lila *(blissful sport) with the gopis consists of dancing in a circle in a particular way, accompanied by music.*

*The key episode of the **Ramayana** is the kidnapping of Sita by the demon king Ravana, who comes disguised as an ascetic and lures her out of the hut. Garuda, the mythical bird who is a great devotee of Rama, attacks the 10-headed Ravana to save Sita but in vain. Later it is the mortally wounded Garuda who informs Rama about the kidnapping of his wife, Sita.*

Chapter 3

THE EPICS AND THE PURANAS

It soon became necessary to transmit the discovered truths, the changing rules, their validity and relevance to the general masses. In a period when the spoken word dominated, it was the myths—stories of gods and superheroes—which offered the best method of dispersal of discovered truths. Stories could be made to embody the truths by which a culture wished to shape itself, the fate of characters becoming a sort of illustration of what should be done and not done.

The rise of the worship of the great gods can be traced through the mythological developments in the two epics, the *Ramayana* and the *Mahabharata,* and in the Puranas. These texts, which achieved their final form in the Gupta age, are gigantic compilations of myths glorifying the acts of a personal deity operating for the benefit of a true devotee.

By the time the Puranas came to be written, the concept of the Hindu trinity, with Brahma as the creator, Vishnu as the preserver and Shiva as the destroyer, had already taken shape. In the popular mind Brahma tended to fade away as the created world was already in place. Vishnu and Shiva continued to reign supreme.

THE EPICS

The *Mahabharata* is an awesome work consisting of about 200,000 lines of 16 syllables each. Said to be the longest poem in the world, it is eight times the size of the *Illiad* and the *Odyssey* put together.

On the text as we know it today there is a general agreement that the oldest portions date back to about the 4th century BC while additions were made till as late as the 4th century AD. The *Mahabharata* encompasses the ritual tradition of the Vedas and the Brahmanas and the mysticism of the Upanishads. It looks forward to the Puranas—the texts that delineate fully the

Despite all this, the text has a unity of sorts, which erudite scholars have noticed and commented on. Van Butenein introduces his translation of the *Mahabharata* as follows: 'However fortuitous its career of expansion, the epic is not an accident of literary history. The grand framework was a design' (*The Mahabharata*).

The most influential Indian work on literary unity, comparable in stature to Aristotle's *Poetics* in the Western tradition, is

During the Dussehra festival, Ram Lilas are enacted across the country in almost every locality. Characters dressed in elaborate costumes and with masks act out scenes from Lord Rama's life.

mythologies related to Hindu gods and goddesses.

Such a process of composition, spread across 800 years, makes sense if we look at the *Mahabharata* not as a single text but as a great compilation. The 'fixed' thematic concern of the text can be said to be the war of succession fought between cousins—the Kauravas and the Pandavas. But the telling of this tale takes up only about a quarter of the book. The rest of the text contains extended discourses on cosmology, ethics, philosophy, statecraft and folklore. The *Mahabharata* itself boasts, 'What is not here is nowhere else.'

Anandvardhan's *Dhvanyaloka*, written in Kashmir in the second half of the 9th century AD. And just as Aristotle uses *The Oedipus* by Sophocles to illustrate his concept of tragedy, for Anandvardhan the *Mahabharata* is the only example of a work that fulfils in its entirety the demanding requirements of poetic unity as he conceives it.

While Western scholars often think of the *Mahabharata* as an epic about war, Indian scholars have always classified it as part of that literature essentially concerned with issues relating to *dharma*. The composition, transmission and reception of the *Mahabharata* has ensured that the epic exists at two levels. At the more obvious level it tells a stirring story of family rivalry and the 18-day war. But at a deeper, more hidden level it tells the story of the struggles of the Brahmins between 400 BC and AD 400, as they sought to retain their hold over the domain of values in the name of *dharma*.

The epic traces the rivalry between the Pandavas and the Kauravas from early childhood to the final conflagration at the end of the 18-day war. The Pandavas eventually emerge victorious and Yudhisthira is crowned king of Hastinapura.

The end of the story, full of grandeur and tenderness, illustrates this. It also embodies, as few other episodes in Indian mythology have done, the Hindu understanding of the concept of *dharma*.

After ruling for many years Yudhisthira abdicates his throne and departs with his brothers for the Himalayas in order to reach the heaven of Indra on Mount Meru. A dog follows the pilgrims from Hastinapura, but so do their sins and moral defects, and these now prove fatal. The first to fall by the wayside is Draupadi, for 'too great was her love for Arjuna'. Next is Sahadeva as he 'esteemed none equal to himself'. Then comes Nakula, as 'ever was the thought in his heart, there is none equal in beauty to me'. Arjuna's turn comes next, due to his boast which he could not fulfil: 'In one day I could destroy all my enemies.' When Bhima falls, he enquires the reason for his fall and he is told: 'When thou gazest on thy foe, thou hast cursed him with thy breath, therefore thou fallest today.' Yudhisthira proceeds alone with the dog until he reaches the gates of heaven. He is invited by Indra but he refuses to enter unless his brothers and Draupadi are also allowed to enter: 'Not even into thy heaven would I enter if they were not there.' He is assured that they are already there and he is again told to enter. Wearing his body of flesh, he again refuses to enter unless his faithful dog is allowed in also. Indra expostulates in vain

as Yudhisthira refuses to abandon his faithful dog. He is at length admitted but there, to his dismay, he finds Duryodhana and his enemies, not his brothers or Draupadi. He refuses to remain in heaven without them and is conducted to the jaws of hell where he beholds terrific sights, and hears laments of grief and anguish. He recoils but well known voices implore him to remain and assuage their sufferings. He triumphs in this crowning trial and resolves to share the fate of his friends in hell rather than abide with their foes in heaven. Having endured this supreme test, the whole scene is shown to be the effect of *maya* or illusion, and Yudhisthira, his brothers and friends dwell with Indra in full glory of heaven forever.

The *Ramayana* is shorter than *Mahabharata*, more elaborate in its poetry, and more consistent in its theme. The *Ramayana* celebrates the life and exploits of Rama, said to be the seventh *avtara* of Lord Vishnu.

The story of Rama has been briefly told in the 'Vana Parva' of the *Mahabharata*, but it is the main subject of the epic written by the sage Valmiki. It is supposed to have been composed around the 5th century BC, but it received its present form a century or two later.

Rama in the story is the epitome of all the virtues, an example to all people of honour, courage and loyalty. He cheerfully accepts exile and never gives way to rage and self pity. The story has had a strong ethical influence on the whole of the land.

The *Ramayana* is divided into seven *khandas* or sections and contains about 500,000 lines. The story of Rama belongs to the heroic incarnation of Vishnu. As Krishnamurthy points out, Rama is *sumukhah*, which simply means he has a good face. This refers to more than his physical features. It refers to the fact that Rama remained unperturbed even in the most trying circumstances. He was all set to be instituted as the crown prince, but by the dawn of the next day he had been told to renounce the kingdom in favour of Bharat, his half brother. Successively Rama proceeded on a 14-year exile. In both circumstances Rama displayed perfect equanimity. Rama is also the ideal hero of the *Gita*. He is said to be *suvrata*. *Vrata* in Sanskrit means a vow, a penance or a purificatory rite. When the *vrata* is great and unexcelled it is said to be *suvrata*. What was the *vrata* of Lord Rama? It was to give protection to those who sought it from him. He gave protection to Sugriva at the cost of his own reputation. He gave protection to Vibhishan against the advice of almost everyone who wished him well. He even gave protection to a crow against his own arrow.

It was Rama's *vrata* to be completely responsible to his people, writes Krishnamurthy. When he decided to abandon Sita (whom he knew to be completely innocent) because of the accusations of an ordinary subject, even his loyal brother Lakshmana had trouble accepting his decision. Rama's reasoning was that any blemish to the throne is more important than personal happiness. He chose to forsake his guiltless beloved rather than forsake his kingly *dharma*.

PURANAS

While the epics treat of the legendary actions of heroes as mortal men, the Puranas celebrate the power and work of the gods. The Puranas are regarded as the unofficial scriptures of modern Hinduism. They centre on the divinities—Vishnu, Shiva, and Shakti.

The term 'purana' means ancient and the texts, said to number eighteen, are a compendia of religious, secular and mythical information on five topics: the creation of the cosmos; the re-creation of the cosmos after its periodic dissolution and disruption; the genealogies of gods and sages; the ages of the worlds and their rulers; and the genealogies of great kings.

Some of them do treat these subjects. Others do not. However, they contain everything else: stories, rituals, moral lectures, recipes, medical advice, philosophy and specialized subjects, such as architecture, iconography, and veterinary information about horses and elephants.

The Puranas are impossible to date with accuracy, but some are obviously older than the others. The essential core of several Puranas was composed during the Gupta period (the 4th to 6th century AD), but over the centuries additions continued to be made and most of them reached their present state only in the 12th century before the arrival of the Moghuls.

The most important of the Puranas are Vayu, Vishnu, Agni and Bhagvata Purana. The others bear the names of different *avtaras* of Vishnu. Unlike the epics the Puranas are definitely sectarian in nature, devoting themselves to the praise of the chosen deity.

The Authors of the Mahabharata *and the* Ramayana

Valmiki

Tradition has it that Valmiki, the author of the *Ramayana*, was originally called Ratnakar. He was by profession a robber and plunder was his vocation. One day, however, he met the divine sage Narada, who asked him to find out whether his family members would accept a share of the

enlightened sage who eventually authored the *Ramayana*. He is also widely known as the Adi Kavi or the 'Original Poet'.

Ved Vyasa

Tradition credits Ved Vyasa, son of sage Parashar, with four monumental achievements that have shaped Hinduism.

Valmiki said that he composed his musical epic, the **Rama-yana**, *to reinforce the Vedic teachings.*

Ved Vyasa said that he specially composed the **Maha-bharata** *to broadcast the Vedic lore to the people at large.*

sins that he was committing for their sake as a robber. Ratnakar asked each of his family members, but they all refused outright to share his burden of sin. This opened the eyes of the robber who came back to Narada, seeking his guidance. Narada asked the illiterate robber to simply repeat the name of 'Rama' continuously. Ratnakar proceeded to do this for many years and years, to the exclusion of everything else, so much so that his body became covered by mounds of anthills. It was Narada himself who came back years later and brought Ratnakar out of the anthills. Hence the name Valmiki, meaning one who has emerged from the anthills. Transformed by the power of faith, Valmiki went on to become an

He is said to have divided, codified and edited the Vedas and the Upanishads, preserving their wisdom, even in the degenerate Kali Yuga in which we are now living. He is said to have composed the philosophical *Brahma Sutra*, which distils the essence of the Upanishads in 555 brief aphorisms. The 18 Puranas, which are encyclopedic collections of myths and legends, are also attributed to him. Finally, he is said to have composed the longest book on earth, the *Mahabharata*—a hundred thousand verse-long epic, which includes the *Bhagvad Gita*, probably the most significant religious text for the modern Hindu.

The four sons of King Dashratha, Rama, Lakshmana, Bharat and Shatrughan grew up together at Ayodhya. While they were still young, the sage Vishvamitra sought the aid of Rama for killing the female demon Taraka, in return for which he gave Rama many celestial weapons. He also took him to the court of Janaka, the lord of Mithila. There Rama won the hand of the lovely Sita, after bending and breaking the bow of Shiva.

Back in Ayodhya, just when Rama was about to be appointed the heir-apparent to the throne, Kekayi, the second wife of king Dashratha, prompted and tutored by her evil maid Manthara, conspired to have Rama sent on a 14-year exile and have her son, Bharat, installed on the throne instead.

Rama departed with his wife Sita and his brother Lakshmana. Soon after his departure King Dashratha died, but Bharat refused to ascend the throne. Instead, he set out to persuade Rama to come back. But Rama declined to return, saying he had to fulfil his dead father's wishes. At length it was arranged that in Rama's absence Bharat would rule over Ayodhya as his vice-regent. He brought back Rama's slippers which were placed upon the throne as a symbol of Rama's supremacy.

In the forest Rama moved from hermitage to hermitage and at length he came to Panchvati on the river Godavari. Here Sarupnakah, Ravana's sister, saw Rama and fell in love with him. Rama repelled her advances, and in her jealousy she attacked Sita. This enraged Lakshmana who cut off her ears and nose. Sarupnakah brought her brothers, Dushana and Khara, along with an army of demons to avenge her, but they were all defeated and chased back by Rama and Lakshmana.

Sarupnakah went back and complained to Ravana in Lanka, who came to Rama's hermitage disguised as an ascetic and kidnapped Sita. Rama and Lakshmana went in pursuit of Ravana. En route they helped king Sugriva to recover his capital Kishkindhya from his usurping brother Bali. This earned Rama not only the support of all the forces of Sugriva and his allies, but

36

King of Ayodhya

also the active aid of Hanuman, the son of the god of wind and Sugriva's general.

Hanuman's devotion to Rama and his extraordinary powers proved invaluable in the campaign against Ravana. He first discovered exactly where Ravana had hidden Sita and later guided the armies of Rama and Sugriva to Lanka. By a superhuman effort a bridge was built over the ocean and Rama's army invaded Ravana's Lanka. After many fiercely contested battles, Lanka was taken, Ravana killed and Sita rescued.

Sita then proceeded to demonstrate her innocence by undertaking the ordeal of fire. She entered the flames in the presence of men and gods, and Agni, the god of fire, led her forth and placed her in Rama's arms unhurt. The war, though fought for the recovery of Sita, symbolizes the victory of good over evil.

The 14 years having ended, Rama triumphantly returned to Ayodhya to be reunited with his brothers and family and to be crowned the king of Ayodhya. His subsequent reign is called Ram Rajya. Perfect in every way, it is the Indian equivalent of the golden age.

However, when a lowly washerman criticized Rama for taking his wife back he resolved to send her to the hermitage of Valmiki. There she gave birth to her twin sons, Luv and Kush. When they were about 15 years, they wandered accidentally into Ayodhya. Rama recognized and acknowledged them and recalled Sita, asking her to prove her innocence once and for all. In a public assembly she declared her purity and called upon the earth to verify her words. It did so. The ground opened beneath her feet and mother earth received her daughter, Sita.

Unable to live without Sita, Rama decided to leave the world. With great state and ceremony he walked into the waters of River Saryu. The voice of Brahma hailed him from the high heavens as he passed into the glory of Vishnu.

Rama and Lakshmana greet the monkey king Sugriva, his general Hanuman and other monkey warriors. It was with the help of the monkey army of Sugriva that Rama invaded Ravana's Lanka and rescued his wife, Sita.

The divine attributes of Hinduism's male deities are symbolized in their figurative representations. Shiva has three eyes, a topknot studded with a crescent moon, and is sometimes shown as half-man, half-woman (ardhnarishvara). Ganesha has an elephant's head, Brahma has four faces, Rama is sumukhah or good-faced. Krishna is variously shown as Arjuna's charioteer, the Supreme God, or as a cowherd.

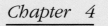

Chapter 4

MALE DIVINITIES
AND SECTS

The emergence of *bhakti* and the absorption into Hindu ritual of newer, more popular local deities led to the decline in the popularity of some of the older Vedic deities and the increase in popularity of others.

THE GODS

Vishnu

Vishnu, a minor deity in the Vedic period, rose to become one of the three great gods of Hinduism. He appears briefly in the ancient hymns sometimes as a sort of helper of the great god Indra and sometimes in his own right as the 'wide striding' one. In Vedic literature he is famous for his three great strides, with which he encompasses the entire universe—the earth, the atmosphere and the heavens.

The etymology of his name conveys the ability to 'spread' or 'extend'. The root *vish* means to pervade and it is this ability that eventually makes him a god of universal dimensions responsible for the preservation of the cosmos. To use a typically Hindu scheme of classification, he is a *sattvik* god, embodying qualities of kindness, mercy and goodness, while committed to playing the role of the preserver. He is often shown as shrewd or cunning, willing to compromise on the means to achieve the ends. In pictures he is represented as a handsome young prince with four hands. One hand holds *panchajanya* (the conchshell), another the *sudarshan chakra,* the third a *gada* or club, called Kaumodaki, and the fourth the *padma* or lotus. He has a bow called Sarnga, and a sword called Nandaka. On his breast is the peculiar mark called Srivatsante, the jewel Kaustubha, and on his wrist is the jewel Syamantaka. He is sometimes represented seated on a lotus with Lakshmi besides him, or reclining on a leaf. Sometimes he is represented in human form while resting on the serpent Sesha.

Of the ten incarnations of Vishnu, the first five are regarded as purely mythological, while in the next three the heroic element predominates. In the ninth *avtara* the religious aspect predominates. The tenth *avtara* of Vishnu is yet to appear. According to the Matsya Purana, there is a reason for the manifold and varied appearances of this deity. To protect Indra and his gods, Vishnu had to kill the mother of Sakura (the teacher of the Asuras), who was also the wife of Brighu, the ascetic. In retaliation, Brighu cursed

Vishnu symbolizes the qualities of permanence, continuity and preservation. In the **Mahabharata** *Vishnu became identified with the more martial aspects of Krishna.*

This is the position he assumes during periods of temporary annihilation of the universe. Sometimes he is shown riding on the gigantic bird Garuda. The holy river Ganga is said to spring from the feet of Vishnu.

Vishnu's preserving powers are embodied in his *avtaras*, or incarnations, in whom his divine essence is represented in different earthly forms. The Vishnu *avtaras*, possessed of superhuman powers, manifest themselves in order to bring about some great good in the world or to correct some great evil. Vishnu is said to have ten *avtaras* of which one is yet to appear.

Vishnu, condemning him to be born ten times amongst men.

The nine *avtaras* of Vishnu which have already appeared are: Matsya, the Fish; Kurma, the Tortoise; Varaha, the Boar; Narasimha, the Man-Lion; Vamana, the Dwarf; Parsuram or Rama with the Axe; Lord Rama, the King of Ayodhya; Lord Krishna; and Buddha, the Teacher.

1. **The Matsya Incarnation:** Vishnu is believed to have incarnated himself as Matsya when Vaivaswata, the seventh Manu and the progenitor of the human race, was under threat of destruction by

a deluge. Vishnu came to Manu in the form of a small fish and asked for protection. Manu guarded and cared for the fish. The fish grew rapidly, till it became so big that only the ocean could contain it. It then told Manu to prepare for the approaching cataclysmic floods. When the floods began, Manu embarked on a ship with all the *rsis* as well as the seeds of all existing life. Vishnu then appeared as a gigantic fish with a huge horn to which Manu tied his ship till the flood waters abated.

of the gods and bearer of the cup of *amrita*; Lakshmi, the goddess of fortune and beauty and the chief consort of Vishnu; Sura, the goddess of wine; Rambha, the ideal woman; Ucha, the wonderful horse; Kaustubha, a celebrated jewel; Airvata, a perfect elephant; *shankah*, the eternal conch of victory; *dhanush*, a famous bow; and *visha*, a poison.

3. **The Varaha Incarnation:** To recover the earth which a demon named Hiranyaksha had dragged to the bottom

Whenever the forces of evil began to rule the world, Lord Vishnu left the heavens and descended on Earth in different forms to rescue mankind. The first four incarnations of Vishnu, symbolizing the wild stage of mankind, were half-man and
a) half-fish,
b) half-tortoise,
c) half-boar,
d) half-lion.

2. **The Kurma Incarnation:** During the Satya Yuga, Vishnu appeared in the form of a tortoise to recover some things of value which had been lost in the previous deluge. Being a tortoise, he placed himself at the bottom of the ocean and made his back the base or pivot of the mountain called Mandara. The gods and demons twisted the serpent Vasuki around the mountain, and each side, using one end of the snake as a rope, churned the sea until they recovered the desired objects. These were *amrita*, the nectar of immortality; Dhanwantari, the physician

of the sea, Vishnu assumed the form of a boar. After a contest that lasted a thousand years, he slew the demon and raised the earth above the sea.

4. **The Narasimha Incarnation:** Vishnu assumed this fearsome form to rid the world of the tyranny of the demon king Hiranyakashipu and to vindicate the faith of one of his greatest *bhakta's* ever—the child Prahalada.
Hiranyakashipu had won a boon from Brahma which had made him invincible so that no human being, god or beast could kill him. This demon's son, named Prahalada, worshipped Vishnu,

which so incensed his father that he tried to kill him, but Prahalada, being under the protection of Vishnu, survived all assassination attempts. Derisively dismissing his son's claim about the omnipresence and omnipotence of Vishnu, Hiranyakashipu demanded to know if Vishnu was present in a stone pillar of the hall, and struck it violently. To avenge Prahalada and to vindicate his own offended majesty, Vishnu emerged from the pillar as Narasimha,

The fifth incarnation of Vishnu as Vamana, or the dwarf, symbolizes the underdeveloped stage of mankind.

half-man and half-lion, and tore the arrogant demon-king to pieces.

5. **The Vamana Incarnation:** The origin of this incarnation is the 'three strides of Vishnu' mentioned in the Rig Veda. In the Treta Yuga or second age, the demon Bali had acquired dominion over the three worlds by his austerities, and the gods were shorn of their power and dignity. To remedy this Vishnu took the form of the diminutive dwarfed son of Kashyapa and Aditi. The dwarf appeared before Bali and begged him to give him as much land as he could step on in three paces. The generous monarch complied with the request. The dwarf, in two strides, covered heaven and earth, but, respecting the virtues of Bali, abstained from stepping

over Patala, the infernal region below the ground. This was left as the domain of Bali and his demons.

6. **The Parsuram or Ram with the Axe Incarnation:** The sixth *avtara* of Vishnu, a Brahmin, was born as the fifth son of sage Jamad-agni and his spouse, Renuka. He appeared at the beginning of the Treta Yuga, to overthrow the tyranny of the Kshatriya race. His story symbolizes a severe power struggle that is believed to have

In his sixth incarnation as Parsuram, Vishnu is shown in complete human form for the first time, with an axe in his right hand.

taken place between the two dominant castes—the Brahmins and the Kshatriyas. The hostilities are said to have begun when Karata-virya, a Kshatriya king, visited the hermitage of Jamad-agni and despite being hospitably entertained, carried off the sacrificial calf. This enraged Parsuram who pursued and killed Karata-virya. But Karata-virya's son, in retaliation, killed Jamad-agni, Parsuram's father. For this murder, Parsuram vowed eternal vengeance against the whole of the Kshatriya race and twenty-one times he cleared the earth of the Kshatriyas, filling the five large lakes of Kurukshetra with their blood. He then retired to Mount Mahendra. Parsuram finds mention in both the *Mahabharata* as well as in the *Ramayana*. In the *Mahabharata* he instructs Arjuna in the use of arms and also puts a curse on Karna, causing his death. He also fights an epic duel with Bhishma, which neither of them win. Both Arjuna and Karna are believed to have visited Parsuram during his retirement to Mount Mahendra.

In the *Ramayana,* where both the *avtaras* of Vishnu are supposed to figure, Parsuram, the earlier *avtara*

rakshasa king of Lanka. His story is briefly mentioned in the *Mahabharata,* but it is given full length treatment in the *Ramayana.* In the sixteenth century, Tulsi Das, a poet saint wrote the *Ramcharita Manas,* based on the story of Rama, in vernacular Hindi. For the Hindus it became the single-most important mythological or religious text.

8. **The Lord Krishna Incarnation:** Krishna is surely the most popular of the Vishnu *avtaras* and has acquired

The seventh incarnation of Vishnu as Rama is a comparatively minor one in which Rama's chief task is to kill a ten-headed demon, Ravana, and rescue his wife Sita from the latter. This story of Rama has deeply influenced the Hindu psyche.

appears in the role of an antagonist of Rama, the later *avtara.* The *Ramayana* makes Parsuram the follower of Shiva and relates how he was angry with Rama for having broken the bow of Shiva. He then challenges Rama to a trial of strength which ends in Parsuram's defeat.

7. **The Lord Rama Incarnation:** Rama, the eldest son of Dashratha, king of the solar race and the ruler of Ayodhya, was Vishnu's seventh incarnation. He is supposed to have appeared at the conclusion of the Treta Yuga to end the menace of Ravana, the all-powerful

such prominence that he is often looked upon not as an incarnation but as the perfect manifestation of Vishnu.

9. **The Buddha Incarnation:** Buddha's great success as a religious teacher induced the Brahmins to incorporate him in the Hindu fold, rather than treat him as an adversary. In a masterly strategic reversal of roles, Vishnu, as Buddha, was depicted as one who deliberately taught wicked men to reject the Vedas, despise the Brahmins and deny the existence of god, to bring about their (the wicked men's) own destruction.

10. **The Kalki Incarnation:** This *avtara* of Vishnu is yet to appear. Seated on a white horse, with a blazing sword in his hand, he will appear at the end of the Kali Yug for the final destruction of evil forces and for the complete restoration of purity and justice.

Shiva

Shiva signifies the auspicious and the gracious. The third great god of the Hindu

his body. His three eyes and the trident in his hands signify that the three great attributes that constitute creation, the *gunas* are united in him.

Shiva's rise to pre-eminence presents a fascinating picture of the synthesis of Aryan and pre-Aryan practices. In all probability Shiva was a powerful non-Aryan god who was later incorporated into the Aryan fold. He is not even mentioned in the Rig Veda. The only Vedic god with whom he can be linked is Rudra, a minor

The Krishna or eighth incarnation, is also the most important of the ten incarnations of Vishnu. This incarnation shows all those aspects of human development associated with childhood, adolescence and adulthood.

trinity, Shiva expresses his divinity through five different kinds of activities: creation, preservation, destruction, the granting of yogic powers and salvation.

Shiva is worshipped both as a great ascetic as well as a householder. As an ascetic he is said to reside on Mount Kailash but as a householder, married to Parvati (or Uma), the daughter of the Himalayas, he is said to live in the city of Varanasi. He has two sons—Ganesha, the elephant-headed deity, and Kartikeya, whose popularity as a deity has waned in recent times. He is surrounded by a host of fierce attendants and has snakes wrapped around

deity in the Rig Veda, as one of Shiva's many later appellations is Rudra, the Lord of Wrath.

Facing page: Almost 2,500 years ago Buddha preached his first sermon in a tiny hamlet near Varanasi and launched a major world religion. In India the high point of Buddhism was the reign of the Mauryan Emperor Ashoka (272-232 BC) and it continued to be the dominant religion for the next few centuries. However, from the eighth century AD onwards Hinduism began to regain its former position with the great Hindu preacher Shankaracharya playing a crucial role in its revival. Buddhism has few followers in India today.

Significantly, one of Shiva's many names is also Pashupati and as Pashupati he bears a remarkable resemblance to the deity represented on a seal found in Mohenjo-daro. This seal shows a god seated in the traditional posture of a yogi, surrounded by an elephant, a tiger, a rhinoceros and a buffalo and it immediately brings to mind the traditional image of Mahadeva Shiva.

The Shiva mythology conveys memories of a time when Shiva was not easily accepted by the Brahmins. There are various ancient Sanskrit tales which describe how the Brahmins initially tried to resist Shiva but finally had to recognize his supremacy. The following story is repeated in various forms. Shiva comes to the forest abode of the Brahmin priests. His sexual magnetism is so overwhelming that all the Brahmin wives succumb to it. The Brahmins are infuriated by this and want to drive Shiva out but eventually have to accept him as a great god and pay him homage. In all probability this reflects historical reality because many Aryans married non-Aryan women who, even in their new households, possibly continued to worship the god of their ancestors.

Even after Shiva had been accepted in the Hindu fold it seems his worship was resisted by the orthodox upper classes. A famous story (in *Kashi Khanda*) celebrates a great king who organized a *yagna*—an elaborate religious ceremony involving sacrifice—to which he invited all the gods except Shiva. In the assembly he explained why he had excluded Shiva. His speech gives an insight into the contradictions and paradoxes that constitute Shiva.

> What is his lineage and what is his clan? What place does he belong to and what is his nature?
> What does he do for a living and how does he behave, this fellow who drinks poison and rides a bull?
> He is not an ascetic, for how can one who carries a weapon be an ascetic? He is not a householder, for he lives in the cremation ground. He is not a

brahmachari (celibate) for he has a wife. And he cannot be a forest dweller, for he is drunk with the conceit of his lordship.
> He is not a Brahmin, for the Vedas do not know him as one. Since he carries a spear and trident, he might be a Kshatriya, but he is not. Since he delights in the destruction of the world, he cannot be a Kshatriya who protects the world from harm. And how can he be a Vaishya, for he has never any wealth. He is not even a Shudra, for he wears snakes as the sacred thread. So he is beyond caste *(varna)* and the stages of life *(ashrams)*. Everything is known by its original source, but Shiva, the immovable, has no original source.
> He is not a man because half his body is female. And yet he is not a woman because he has a phallus. He is not even a eunuch because his phallus is worshipped. He is not a boy for he is great in years and he is proclaimed in the world as beginningless he is so ancient. Yet he is not old for he is without old age and death.

(from DIANA ECK,
BANARAS: CITY OF LIGHT: 99-100)

By AD 1000 Shiva had been accepted as a god by the Aryans. With him also came modes of worship that were alien to the Aryans. The non-Aryans practised fertility cults and worshipped female deities as well as the phallus. As Shiva became dominant, worship of both was incorporated into Hinduism.

The Shiva *linga* is the most commonly seen symbol of Shiva. It consists of a cylindrical black stone set in a circular base. It has definite sexual connotations though as has been pointed out by scholars it is a bi-sexual rather than a merely phallic symbol. The erect shaft represents the male aspect of Shiva while the circular base represents Shakti, Shiva's female half. The *linga* as a Shiva symbol represents the fact that Shiva cannot be seen in terms of gender divisions. One of his names is Ardhanarishvara, the 'Half-Woman Lord' and sometimes he is represented as a one-breasted deity, clad half in a sari and half in a dhoti.

Though the sexual aspect of the *linga* cannot be overlooked, its significance as a sexual symbol has diminished. It is now considered more an emblem of a god who is beyond human comprehension. As a symbol it represents the wholeness of the Hindu world view.

In Hindu thought and mythology, two forces interact in constantly shifting balance, approximating but never attaining the point

and peace' (*Siva: The Exotic Ascetic:* 312).

The *linga* in its totality is seen as a symbol in which these two forces are in perfectly balanced tension. The circular base representing *shakti* embodies *pravritti*, the energy of life leading to evolution of the One into the multiplicity of the created universe. The erect pole represents the still centre of the turning world, the involution of the multiplicity back into the One. Metaphorically speaking, everything in the world is said to exist in the *linga*.

Shiva, the third God of the Hindu trinity, has three eyes, the third one (between the eyebrows) being usually closed except at the time of destruction of things. In his form as the Supreme Being (Mahadeva) *he is represented in the phallic symbol.*

of simultaneous existence of the two extremes. These two forces are termed *pravritti* (energy, activity, worldly involvement) and *nivritti* (quiescence, withdrawal, release). A very perceptive scholar of Hinduism, W. D. O'Flaherty comments: 'One attempt to make the Universe intelligible regards it as an eternal rhythm playing and pulsing outward from spirit to matter *(pravritti)* and then backwards and inwards from matter to spirit *(nivritti)* . . . The Tantras recognize and consecrate both movements, the outward throbbing stream of energy and enjoyment and the calm returning flow of liberation

Though the main focus of Shiva worship is the *linga*, anthropomorphic images of the god as visualized by folk artists can be seen on walls, temples and homes. The most common of these is Shiva sitting cross-legged in the posture of a yogi on a tiger skin. He has three eyes. The *naga* (serpent) is his necklace, while the Ganga flows from his head. His drum and

Following pages 48-49: *A profusion of Shiva* lingas, *each of which has been installed by some devotee in memory of the dead. Here we are at the Jangambari Math in Varanasi, the headquarters of the Virshaiva sect.*

his trident are either in his hands or by his side. He may wear the crescent moon as an ornament and he might be carrying the skull in his hand, or have a necklace of skulls around his throat. Sometimes he is accompanied by Parvati, at other times he is shown sitting alone in the Himalayas.

The essence of Shiva is the transcendence of all the paradoxes that limit existence. He is the great god who confounds and contradicts human categories and conventions. He is both an ascetic and a householder, both man and woman, creator and destroyer, both Dionisian and Apollian. His name means 'the auspicious one' but he haunts cremation grounds, anoints his body with the ashes of the dead, wears the moon (but also snakes) as ornaments. He drinks *bhang* (an inebriating brew), capers around with an unruly bunch of followers, so much so that he is considered mad, and yet he is the ultimate yogi, in complete control of himself: O'Flaherty writes:

> The mediating principle that tends to resolve all oppositions is . . . Shiva himself. Among ascetics he is a libertine and among libertines he is an ascetic; conflicts which they cannot resolve, or can attempt to resolve only by compromise, he simply absorbs into himself . . . Shiva is particularly able to mediate in this way because of his protean character; he is all things to all men. He merely brings to a head the extreme and therefore least reconcilable aspects of the oppositions which, although they may be resolved in various ways on the divine level, are almost never reconciled on the human level (Ibid.: 36).

Brahma

Brahma, the supreme deity of the Brahmanas and the Upanishads, often considered to be the first member of the Hindu trinity, is not popularly worshipped by the modern Hindu. The town of Pushkar near Ajmer in Rajasthan is the only place where a major temple devoted to this deity exists. Like a family elder, in the rush of current events he has been partly forgotten.

However, his name is invoked often enough and he continues to play a major role in the Hindu religious imagination as the creator of the universe. The traditional Hindu concept of time is structured according to the day and the night of Brahma.

A waking day of Brahma is said to last for 2,160,000,000 human years. The created

In the Upanishads Brahma, the supreme creative spirit, is seen as universal and forming the elemental matter from which everything originally emerged.

world survives only as long as Brahma stays awake. When he sleeps, and his night is as long as his day, then the world comes to an end, though the Vedas, the sages and the gods in heaven survive. When he wakes up again he restores creation and this process is repeated again and again.

Brahma is often represented with four heads though he originally had five. One of his heads was destroyed by Shiva, who had been insulted by him. He is shown to have four arms. He holds a spoon, a string of beads or his bow, his water jug and the Vedas. His consort, though she is not often shown with him, is Saraswati, the goddess of learning. His vehicle is the Hansa-Vahana or the swan chariot.

Ganesha

If Brahma is not as popular today as he once was, Ganesha, the elephant-headed deity is becoming more and more popular everyday. He is the remover of obstacles and it is to him that one must turn if one wants any new enterprise that one might have launched to be successful. Before the start of every Hindu religious ceremony, Ganesha's presence has to be invoked and his blessings sought.

In mythical terms, Ganesha is regarded

One of the most popular deities, Ganesha, the 'remover of obstacles', is worshipped at the start of a ritual or journey. His images are found in practically every household.

as the eldest son of Shiva and Parvati and he is considered to be the head of Shiva's *ganas*—the many minor deities who attend upon Shiva.

There are many legends which give an account of his origin and seek to explain how he acquired his elephant head. According to one popular and widely known story he was created by Parvati from a portion of her own body to act as her bodyguard. Once when she went bathing she told him to guard the door and to let no one enter. However, it so happened that it was Shiva himself who wished to enter, but Ganesha would not let him, so Shiva cut off his head. When Parvati remonstrated, Shiva brought him back to life, replacing his head with that of

an elephant. Another legend has it that once Shiva and Parvati saw a male and female elephant cavorting on a full moon night. They changed themselves into elephants and so Ganesha was born. According to yet another legend, the gods created Ganesha, the lord of obstacles, to put hindrances in the way of demons, who were becoming increasingly popular.

Ganesha is also credited with writing the *Mahabharata* on the dictation of Vyasa (the author) and so is specially propitiated by authors embarking on a new book.

There are numerous Ganesha temples all over the country and almost every village has a niche where an image of Ganesha is installed and worshipped. In addition, most of the Shiva and Vishnu temples have Ganesha statues. He is often represented as short and fat, with a cheerful, bulging belly and the head of an elephant with only one tusk. In his hands he holds a shell, a discus, a club and a water lily. His vehicle is the rat and sometimes he is depicted riding it.

Hanuman

Hanuman is yet another deity who is increasingly gaining popularity. Students giving exams make a special point of praying to him, for he is renowned for his ability to perform impossible feats.

Said to be the son of Vayu, the god of wind, Hanuman is a prominent character in the *Ramayana*. He is Lord Rama's chief ally and his ideal devotee. His superhuman strength and indomitable will enable him to perform many heroic feats in defence of Rama. When searching for Sita, he jumps from India to Ceylon in one bound. He burns down Ravana's Lanka, uproots and transports an entire mountain to bring a life-saving herb to save the life of Lakshmana, Rama's younger brother. He kills the monster Kala-nemi and returns with Rama to Ayodhya. For his services he receives the boon of perpetual life and youth. Hanuman is often represented with a red monkey face, a strong muscular form and a long tail.

Jagannath

Jagannath, the tutelary deity and lord of Puri is not one of the *avtaras* of Vishnu but he is commonly accepted as an appearance of Vishnu. However it is entirely possible that he was a local divinity whose worship was engrafted on to Hinduism. There are several legends to account for the form in which he is worshipped and for the peculiar sanctity of Puri, the chief place of his worship. One would afterwards obtain a rich reward for his religious deeds. With the help of Vishvakarma, the divine architect, Indradhumn raised a grand temple in the blue mountains of Orissa and then began to make the image. But Brahma promised to make the image famous as it was and he invited all the gods to its inauguration. Thus the fame of Jagannath was established all over the world. Next to him, there is generally an image of Balarama, his brother and Subhadra, his sister.

According to some views the shape of Jagannath's image conforms to a typical Buddhist symbol. This view is confirmed by the fact that Puri was once the head centre of Buddhism.

account says that the king of Puri was apprised in his dream that on a certain day a certain piece of wood will arise from the sea, and that it would be the true form of the deity. The king's dream turned out to be true and when he had collected the idol, he proceeded to house it in a magnificent temple, and named it Jagannath, the ruler of the world. In another account, when Krishna was accidentally shot by the hunter Jaras, his bones were left to rot under the tree till Indradhumn, a king who was earnestly striving to propitiate Vishnu, was directed to form an image to replace the bones, with the assurance that he

Facing page: *Hanuman, the son of Vayu the god of wind, won fame as the helper of Rama. He possessed supernatural strength, could leap through the air, cover great distances and change his shape at will. A very popular deity, specially in the villages, Hanuman is worshipped all over India as the god to whom to turn when in difficulty.*

Following pages 54-55: *Krishna is seen with his favourite consort, Radha, an incarnation of Lakshmi. Radha's love for Krishna is interpreted in mystical terms as the reaching out of the human soul towards god. The Radha-Krishna relationship is thought of as the ideal archetype of the relationship of a god with his true devotee.*

The Jagannath image is worshipped in the temple, but is also taken out once a year in a huge procession called the Rath Yatra. The image is placed in a mighty wheeled carriage made specially for this purpose. The carriage is drawn by vast multitudes of enthusiastic devotees and immense merit is supposed to accrue to those who assist in dragging it.

SECTS

The rise of theism triggered the growth of sectarianism. From AD 300 onwards Vaishnavism or Vishnu theism, Shaivism or Shiva theism and Tantrism, devoted to the worship of goddesses, began to gain in prominence, overshadowing the sectarian worship of other gods and divinities.

At present, devotees of Vishnu, Shiva and the goddesses are divided into numerous sub-sects spread all over the country. These have often been established by inspirational spiritual leaders. However, a common core of beliefs and shared practices enable them to establish their distinctive identity as a Vaishnava, Shaiva or a Tantric sect.

Vaishnavism

Some of the key elements of Vaishnavism are the Bhagvata doctrine, the Pancaratra system and the Gopal-Krishna or the Radha-Krishna cult.

The Vishnu and the Bhagvata Purana describe the story of the cowherd Krishna and also his amorous play with the *gopis*. The Pancaratra Samhitas or collections, said to have been composed between AD 600-800 are said to number 108 texts. Together they give a detailed exposition of the faith of the Vaishnavas.

Pure Vaishnava devotionalism flowered in the south, for the crucial Bhagvata Purana is said to have been composed in Tamil. However, it was the songs of the famous Alwars, the Vaishnava poet-saints, that truly spread the message of Vaishnavism among the masses. Their devotional songs, composed between the fifth and ninth century AD are called *prabandhams* and are at times referred to as the Vaishnava Vedas.

The next landmark in the evolution of Tamil Vaishnavism is the rise of a school of philosophers known as Acharyas. Nathmuni, the first of these, lived in the ninth or tenth century AD. He was a great philosopher and the school he established took up the task of giving a philosophical background to the Vaishnava theories and creeds.

He organized the sect of Sri Vaishnava, and popularized it among the masses by collecting the songs of Alvars, setting them to Dravidian music, and having them sung in temples. The sect survives to this day.

In the eleventh century the school produced the famous philosopher, Ramanuja. His great task was to put the Vaishnava religion as well as the *bhakti* cult on a secure philosophical footing. The doctrine of Advaita propounded by the famous philosopher Shankaracharya directly contradicted the key assumptions of *bhakti*. If there is only one Spirit, and everything else is unreal, there is no scope for personal devotion to the supreme God by the individual, for the two are really one and the same. Basing himself on the Upanishads and the *Brahma Sutra*, Ramanuja thought of the individual soul as a distinct attribute of the supreme Soul. The latter can be an object of devotion. His sect came to be known as Sri Sampradaya which recognizes Sri (Lakshmi), Bhu (earth), and Lila (sport) as consorts of Vishnu.

The philosophy of Ramanuja was further developed by Madhava (13th century) who conceived of God as altogether distinct from the individual spirit. He was the founder of another influential Vaishnava sect, which continues to survive today.

By and large, southern Vaishnavism laid little stress on the cowherd element of Krishna and altogether ignored Radha. Vaishnavism in north India was, however, different. Nimbarka, who lived in Vrindavan sometime in the 12th century, believed God to be both identical and yet distinct from the individual spirit. He differed from the southern Vaishnava sages in giving prominence to the saga of Radha and Krishna. Radha according to him was the eternal consort of Vishnu. Nimbarka's sect, known as Sanaka-sampradaya, flourishes in northern India to this day.

The Radha-Krishna cult was carried to its extreme form by Vallabha (16th century). Elaborate rituals for the worship of Radha

ignored caste distinctions completely. Later Vaishnava preachers like Tukaram, Ramananda, Kabir, Tulsi, Dadu and Makudas continued the tradition of elevating the *bhakti* cult to the highest spiritual plane, based on foundations of morality and equality.

Shaivism

Shaivite theism bases itself on the Puranas (Vayu, Linga, Kurma and so on) and the

The linga *of light that burst forth in Varanasi was the first* linga*, and the world-spanning form of Shiva. Shiva vowed that henceforth this unfathomable* linga *would become small so that the people might use it as a symbol of worship.*

and Krishna, and religious feasts and festivals were fully developed, all marked by a spirit of sportive enjoyment, for the highest spiritual objective is to join in the eternal sport of Radha and Krishna.

Bengal Vaishnavism was deeply influenced by Chaitanya, a contemporary of Vallabha. He elevated the passions of Radha-Krishna to a high spiritual plane. His piety, spiritualism and devotion and his disregard for ceremonies introduced a pure and spiritual element in the Vaishnava tradition. The other notable contribution of Chaitanya was that he began preaching in the vernacular instead of Sanskrit and

Agama texts. There are twenty-eight Agama manuals with a number of sub-texts, the total number of texts approximating two hundred. The Agamas were composed before the seventh century AD.

A unique form of early Shaivism evolved in Kashmir. But later Shaivism flourished in the south due to the devotional Tamil poems of Nayanmars (Shaiva saints). These are divided into eleven collections which, together with the Periya Purana, constitute the foundation of Tamil Shaivism.

The first seven collections, known as Devaram, composed by Saint Sambandar,

Saint Appar, and Saint Sundarar, all of whom wrote in the seventh century AD, are considered to be as auspicious as the Vedas.

The eighth collection, *Tiruvacakam,* of Manikkavacagar and the tenth collection *Tirumandiram* of Tirumular occupy pride of place in Shaiva literature. They reflect the theology of the Agamas and are admired for the beauty of their poetic composition.

The patronage of the later Pallava kings from the sixth century AD onwards and of the mighty Chola emperors proved a great boon to Shaivism in the south.

An important development took place in the thirteenth and fourteenth centuries. This was the rise of Shiva Siddhanta which now replaced the Agamas and laid down the foundation of the new Shaiva system.

A very powerful Shaiva sect known as the Virasaivas or Lingayats rose in Karnataka and Maharashtra. From the twelfth century onwards this one sect flourished at the expense of Jainism and Buddhism and was the main cause of their decline in the south.

The Virshaivas give great importance to the monasteries, for every Lingayat must belong to a monastery and have a guru. They worship Shiva in his phallic form, reject the authority of the Vedas, disbelieve in the doctrine of rebirth and do not believe in Brahminism.

In the north Varanasi emerged as a great centre for Shiva worship. Legend has it that after his marriage to Parvati the divine couple decided to live in Varanasi, promising not to forsake it ever.

Tantrism

Tantra is a generic term referring to the literature of certain religious cults which came into prominence within Hinduism from AD 500 onwards. They comprise esoteric teachings and mystic practices of various kinds and their religious practices include *mantra* (a sacred formula addressed to the deity), *bija* (mystical letter or a syllable or letter which often forms an essential part of the *mantra* and which is given to the disciple by his guru), *yantra* (mystical diagram), *nyasa* (assignment of the various parts of the body to tutelary deities), *mudra* (particular physical positions and hand gestures), *mandala* (mystical diagram without the *bija,* or letters), *yagna* (sacrifice), yoga, and *upasana* (worship).

The Tantras also deal with various details of *puja*, orgiastic rites, temple architecture and iconography. The worship of the female consort of the gods constitutes an important aspect of Tantra worship. Tantras are often inspired by the Samkhya philosophy according to which the Spirit or Purusa, identified either with Shiva or Vishnu, is inactive, while Prakriti, identified with Shakti or Sri, is productive, constituting the first universal material cause. Hence in Tantra worship the female deity often takes precedence over the male counterpart.

Tantric literature does not oppose the Vedas, but it claims that in the Kali Yuga the Vedas do not suffice, and one needs the help of the Tantras to achieve the ultimate goals. Unlike the Brahmanic tradition, the Tantras do not propagate renunciation of the world and its pleasures as the ideal way to achieve the union of Atman and Brahman. Instead they teach liberation through *bhoga* (enjoyment) of physical and emotional pleasures.

The system lays stress on the inherent power of sound and the presence in the human body of a large number of minute channels or threads of occult forces (*nadi*) and six great centres of that force (*chakra*) described as so many lotuses one above the other.

The worship of the goddess Shakti was accompanied by sacrifices of animals and occasionally also human beings. But the most characteristic feature of the cult was the *chakra puja,* that is, circle worship in which an equal number of men and women sit around a circle and utter mystic *mantras*, partaking of the five elements: wine, meat, fish, parched grain and sex. Many sorcerous practices formed part of this cult. Detailed instructions for these practices are given in the Tantra texts. Hence Tantrism is used as a general name for similar rituals which are found in many religious sects.

Taken at its best, the Tantric doctrine stresses the dynamic principle of the origin of the universe and the different deities can be located in different parts of the human body by means of a form of yoga. However for the believers of Tantra, it is not the gods but the goddesses who are the real source of energy and activity in the cosmos. For

Tantra was very popular in the Himalayan belt. When Buddhism reached there, it got integrated with the existing local tantric cult and became 'Greater way' Buddhism. The popularity of Tantra is related to the simplicity of its procedures. It is not time consuming, and a person engrossed in worldly affairs can also pursue the path easily, by devoting a part of his spare time to its practice. Results are seen in a short span of time if a devotee has been assiduous.

A senior ascetic is seen resting while his young disciples keep vigil during the Kumbha Mela. The unwavering faith in the guru *is a binding force in ascetic organizations. It is believed that those who have renounced their homes, broken ties with their kinsmen and caste, should find solace in establishing new ties.*

them, but for the help of the *devi*, the gods themselves can do little.

By worshipping Shakti or any other goddess in the manner indicated above, the devotee seeks to attain by supernatural means and in an incredibly short time spiritual and material benefits. Some Tantras however uphold practices which are revolting and horrible.

Following pages 60-61: *Tantriks performing their esoteric rituals. It is the large concourse of monks and ascetics of diverse orders at the Kumbha Mela that draws millions of religious-minded people from all over the country. The Tantras lay great emphasis on initiation. Some sanyasi sects like the Naga Sadhus, in fact, hold the initiation ceremony of an ascetic into the Naga fold at the Kumbha Mela itself.*

Symbols are an integral part of Hindu religious thought and practice. Over the centuries innumerable symbols have evolved. Some of the most important ones are briefly discussed below.

Tilaka

The *tilaka* is an auspicious mark applied on the *ajna* (spot between the two eyebrows) of the devotee, The form, shape and material used for the *tilaka* differ from sect to sect. Devotees of Shiva apply sacred ashes, those of Vishnu apply sandalwood paste, while worshippers of Shakti apply *kumkuma*. The centre of the forehead is the most important psychic location in the human body and its impor-tance is stressed by putting a co-loured mark at this spot. This is where the sixth *chakra* (centre of occult forces in the body) is believed to be located.

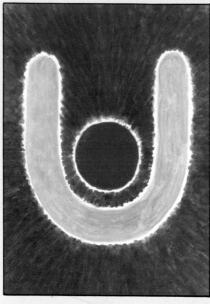

Tilaka

Lotus

The symbol of the lotus *(padma)* is extensively represented in Hindu temple iconography and architecture, and rich meanings are associated with it. Since it is born in water, it is the flower of life blossoming on the creative waters. It is the visible sign of consciousness in matter, and the seat of Brahma. The lotus is also associated with Vishnu since it is said to arise from his divine navel. Lakshmi, the consort of Vishnu, is intimately associated with the lotus, and is often described as

Lotus

'lotus born'. She is the lotus goddess, represented standing on a lotus pedestal, bedecked with lotus garlands. Since the lotus goddess bestows health, pros-perity, long life, and above all, wealth, the symbol of the lotus is associated with all the good things of life, and with self-creation.

Kumbha

Kumbha means pot and it refers to a globular vessel with a constricted neck. It is a symbol of great antiquity as it figures in the Puranic story of the churning of the milk-ocean by demons and gods to retrieve the nectar of immortality. This churning of the ocean, supervised by Vishnu, caused the *kumbha* (containing the nectar) to emerge. As an architectural motif, the *kumbha* occurs in varied form all over India. It is also used in the worship of deities and for decorating temples, cities, and houses on festive or auspicious occasions. Symbolically, the *kumbha* represents the whole of the universe, with the seat of

Kumbha

Symbols

Vishnu located in its mouth, Indra in the neck, Mother Goddess in the centre, Brahma in the root, and the earth, oceans, rivers, mountains and the Vedas at its base. It is also considered the symbol of global welfare as well as of prosperity on earth. It is said to accumulate good deeds and destroy ignoble ones. It is the focal symbol of India's greatest festive gathering, the Kumbha Mela, celebrated once in twelve years.

Chakra

The *chakra* (disc) is a perfect symbol of the cyclical view of life and its rhythmic ebb and flow in a cosmic pattern. It symbolizes the movement that creates and governs both space and time. In Hindu terminology, the cosmos is known as Brahmanda-chakra and the world as Samsara-chakra. The eternal cycle of action and causality is known as Karma-chakra, while time itself is known as the Kala-chakra and the moral order is known as the Dharma-chakra. The *chakra* has been a major symbol since the time of the Rig Veda and is a frequent iconographic motif. Buddhists and Jains traditionally worship the *chakra*. For the Hindus, the Sudarshan-chakra is the chief weapon of the great god Vishnu used for the preservation of the world.

Chakra

Swastika

The *swastika* is a solar symbol. Spreading out in all four directions it symbolizes the cosmos. It derives its auspiciousness from

Swastika

the four-fold principle of divinity. Brahma is said to be four-faced. The four Vedas, four *ashrams*, four *varnas* and the four *purusarthas* are all associated with the *swastika*. The antiquity of this symbol is established by the fact that it has been found engraved on some of the Indus valley seals.

Aum

The single word *aum* is so sacred and auspicious that it is considered to be the most sacred of all the Hindu *mantras*. Used for invocation, benediction, ritual worship, festivals and religious ceremonies, it consists of five separate sounds: 'A' 'U' 'M' plus the nasalization and resonance of the sound. It is said that within the 'Aum' Vishnu is 'A', Brahma is 'U' and Shiva is 'M'; the *bindu* is the trinity in unity while the *nada* symbolizes transcendence. In the Upanishads, however, *aum* is the symbol of the *nirguna* Brahman, without attributes, beyond human consciousness and duality (*pranav*).

Aum

Hinduisms goddesses in their benevolent form are the beautiful and graceful Parvati, Uma, Minaksi (consorts of Lord Shiva), Saraswati (consort of Brahma) and Lakshmi (consort of Vishnu). Subhadra, the sister of Lord Krishna, is worshipped as the sister of Lord Jagannath. Shakti, or the Mother Goddess, is the power aspect of Shiva, often manifested as Bhuvaneswari or Durga, and in the fierce forms as Chandika or Kali.

Chapter 5

FEMALE DIVINITIES

Goddesses have always been part of the religious life of India. In India's earliest civilization in the Indus Valley, goddesses with full breasts, rounded hips, adorned with the hip belt or girdle were found roughly shaped in terracotta. Goddesses of local and regional significance have attracted supplicants asking for their blessings and protection for nearly three thousand years. The word *shakti* came to be used to describe these female divinities. *Shakti* means 'energy' or 'power' and these, indeed are life energies of the world, firmly associated with both nourishment and the vagaries of nature. The rivers of India were praised as mother rivers. The earth was also seen as a female divinity. With Parvati, the wife of Shiva and the daughter of the king of the Himalayas, the mountains too were associated with the goddesses. Finally, local deities presiding over individual towns and villages were predominantly female. Even the great holy cities of India, such as Ayodhya, Ujjain, Varanasi, had female tutelary deities. All these *devis*, embodied in trees, rivers, mountains and towns, were place-specific and often known as *mata* in the north or *amman* in the south.

In the first half of the period stretching from the Mauryan to the Gupta reign, it would not have been meaningful to speak of *the* goddess for there were thousands of goddesses. The second half of this period, however, saw the rise of a larger conception of the *Devi*, of whom these many *devis* were partial manifestations. Early evidence of this process is seen in the *Mahabharata* and the Matsya Purana, where they are all grouped and listed together. The most powerful goddess' shrines came to be seen as the *pithas*, the benches of the respective goddesses.

The great hymn to *devi*, the *Devi Mahatmya*, which appeared in this period, praises the goddess Chandika as the eternally present one, from whom the universe was extended in the beginning. It tells of her gathering up the weapons or the *shaktis* of the male gods in order to slay mighty demons and it calls her by the name of many goddesses: Ambika, Durga, Sri, Gauri. In the wrath of battle, the terrible Kali emerged from Chandika's forehead wearing a garland of skulls, her tongue drooling out for blood. She filled the entire universe with her roar. In the *Devi Mahatmya* it is clear that the goddess Chandika has emerged after gathering together the powers and domains of countless *devis* into a grand theistic vision of a single Mahadevi.

As Mahadevi, Shakti (or the female energy of Shiva) has two characteristics: one mild, the other fierce, and it is under the latter aspect that she is especially worshipped. She has a great variety of names, forms, attributes and actions. In her milder forms she is Uma, Gauri, Parvati, Maimvati and Bhavani. In her terrible form she is Durga, Bhairavi, Kali, Chandi or Chandika.

Uma

Uma appears as the daughter of Daksha, the son of Brahma. She had insisted on marrying Shiva in spite of the fact that her father had objected to the match. She is also known as Sati on account of the fact that when her father deliberately insulted her husband by not inviting him to a major sacrificial ritual, she voluntarily entered the

Uma (light) was Lord Shiva's consort who died in tragic circumstances and was later reborn as Parvati.

sacrificial fire in the presence of the gods and Brahmins.

Parvati

Uma is reborn after death as Parvati and after marrying Lord Shiva again, remains his constant companion. The divine couple is often shown to be in love with each other or shown seated on Mount Kailash discussing the most abstract questions of Hindu philosophy. But on one occasion Shiva is believed to have reproached her for her black skin. This so grieved her that she left her husband and went and performed austerities to Brahma, who, pleased with her, granted her the boon of a golden skin. Hence she came to be known as Gauri.

As Parvati the goddess is the constant companion of Shiva. The couple is often shown seated on Mount Kailash discussing the most abstruse questions of Hindu philosophy.

Saraswati

Saraswati is the goddess of learning and wisdom and is said to be the wife of the supreme creator god, Brahma. However, she is seldom seen with her consort. Often she is represented as a fair, graceful lady with no extra limbs, wearing a slender crescent on her brow, and sitting either on a lotus or on a rock surrounded by swans. In another popular representation, she is sometimes shown sitting on her vehicle, the peacock, at other times she is shown standing on an open lotus, blessing her devotees.

Saraswati, the goddess of speech and learning, is said to have invented the Sanskrit language. She is also the inspirer of the Arts and Sciences.

Always a benevolent deity, her two back hands carry a rosary and a book or a lotus flower, while the two front ones hold a traditional musical instrument—the vina. She presides over the world of learning and is specially honoured by the musicians.

Saraswati has many other names like Brahmi and Vani. Some argue that Gayatri is yet another name of Saraswati and that the famous 'Gayatri Mantra', easily the most famous and the most significant *mantra* in the entire Hindu scripture, is addressed to her.

Saraswati has a strong presence in the Rig Veda. Etymologically, her name means 'to flow on' and can refer both to a river and to the ever-flowing stream of learning, wisdom and eloquence.

It was while the Aryans were living by the river Saraswati that the Rig Veda and many other major Hindu texts were written or compiled in their present form. Since the area was so significant and so closely associated with the composition of the *mantras*, the goddess herself eventually came to be regarded as the inspirer of noble hymns.

As the wife and active energy of Brahma, she is also praised for her work as a creator. In the tenth book of the Rig Veda, she is identified as the supreme creator: 'My origin is in the midst of the ocean; and therefore do I pervade all beings, and touch this heaven with my form. Originating all beings, I pass like a breeze; I am above this heaven, beyond this earth; and who is the great one, so am I.'

Lakshmi

Lakshmi, the goddess of wealth and beauty is pre-eminently the consort of Vishnu. She is one of the fourteen 'gems' to have sprung up, when the gods churned the ocean of milk to procure the nectar of immortality. Lakshmi is also known as Padma or Sri. Unlike Saraswati, she is always seen with her lord and when Vishnu appeared on the earth in the form of Rama, she became Sita, his faithful spouse. In the Krishna *avtara*, she appeared as Rukmini, the most beloved of the lord.

Lakshmi, the wife of the great god Vishnu, is the goddess of fortune who is specially worshipped during Diwali.

As a goddess of wealth and riches, she is sometimes thought to be fickle and temperamental, highlighting the essentially unstable nature of wealth and therefore needs to be propitiated with special care.

She has many forms but she is most often seen as Gaja-Lakshmi, seated in a yogic posture. Her two lower hands carry a conch shell and a bowl of ambrosia, while the other two hands are seen holding lotus flowers. Two elephants are seen sprinkling the goddess with water from their raised trunks.

As the goddess of prosperity Lakshmi presides over marriage ceremonies and is also invoked for the increase of progeny. She is specially worshipped on the last day of the dark night in the month of Kartika or in the month of Ashwin, in the last of the darkening fortnight.

In the Vishnu Purana, a famous hymn is addressed to her by Indra which captures here identity as the popular symbol of beauty and prosperity, lending joy and happiness to the home and the family:

> From thy propitious gaze, oh mighty goddess,
> men obtain wives, children, dwelling, friends, harvest, wealth.
> Health, strength, power, victory, happiness, are easy attainment
> to those upon whom thou smilest.
> Thou art the mother of all beings,
> as the god of gods, Vishnu,
> is their father; and this world,
> whether inanimate or animate,
> is pervaded by thee and Vishnu.

Durga

The goddess, Durga, is the consort of Lord Shiva. When seen with her consort, Durga is shown with only two hands, a beautiful smiling face and wearing her usual ornaments. However, it is when she is worshipped alone that she can be shown in any of the following three forms: mild, benevolent, and fierce. Generally she is shown with four or more hands carrying special weapons and emblems.

The consort of Lord Shiva is known by many names, like Uma, Parvati, Durga, Devi, Kali, Bhawani, Haimwati, Katyayani and Ambika. She is also supposed to be the sister of Vishnu and carries in her hands Vishnu's emblems—the discus and the conch shell. Her images show her standing on the head of a dead buffalo or a lotus

The story of Durga's origin is widely known. When Mahisasura, a mighty demon, defeated Indra, the king of gods after a 100-year war and usurped his throne in

Durga (the inaccessible) is the fierce form of Lord Shiva's consort, and is ardently worshipped in West Bengal.

heaven, the gods, advised by Brahma, went to Vishnu and Shiva to seek out their aid. As the enraged gods sat together, a kind of flame issued from their mouths and from this flame emerged the mighty goddess Durga with ten arms, each arm holding a different weapon.

Mounted on her lion, the goddess confronted the mighty demon who had defeated the gods and a fierce battle ensued. The demon, able to change his form rapidly, eluded the goddess till at length the goddess planted her foot on his head and cut it off with a single stroke of her mighty sword. The demon, however, did not die till Durga put an end to the combat by spearing him through the heart.

The Durga Puja, a major festival in north India, specially in Bengal, commemorates her victory over Mahisasura, and in an oft-seen representation we see the goddess with ten arms trampling upon the demon.

Her other feats include the defeat of the army of Chanda and Munda and also the killing of demons Madhu and Kaitabha who had troubled Brahma.

The first nine nights of the bright half of the month of Ashwin, called Navratri, are specially devoted to the worship of Durga. At first a grand image of the beautiful goddess is prepared. On the fifth day the image is dressed. On the sixth day of the festival she is 'awakened'; the seventh and eighth day are the great days of battle and victory. The next day the image of the goddess is reverentially cast in the river, marking the end of the festival.

Kali

The fearsome Kali is yet another manifestation of the *devi*. Also known as Mahakali or Bhadrakali, these are terrible figurative manifestations showing her with blood red mouth, dishevelled flame-like hair, wearing a necklace of skulls and a girdle of severed arms.

Kali lives either with Shiva on the Himalayas or in her own place in the

Kali (the black one) was originally a name for one of the seven tongues of flame of the god Agni. Later it became the name of the fierce consort of Lord Shiva.

Vindhyas. She is worshipped in the darkest nights of the month and her numerous representations show her riding a bull, either with a trident or serpent bracelet, and a half moon on her forehead. Sometimes she is shown riding a bull with a trident in her hand and a half moon on her forehead. At other times she is shown riding a lion. Her forehead is marked with Shiva's third eye.

In the *Devi Mahatmya*, the goddess is described as an unconquerable warrior who came into existence through the combined anger of all the gods. It is to her credit that she ruthlessly seeks out evil and destroys it.

Representing the principle of darkness, Kali delights in the slaughter of her foes. There are several Kali temple all over India but the most famous one is the Kali temple of Calcutta.

There is a Puranic tale which explains how the important Shakti centres emerged in India. Once upon a time, according to the tale, there ruled a king named Daksha whose youngest daughter wanted to marry Lord Shiva, the mountain ascetic with rather odd living habits. Daksha did not approve of the prospective bridegroom but nevertheless Shiva and Sati did get married.

Later Daksha organized a *yagna* in which all the *devas* and *rsis* were invited but not Shiva. Sati went to the *yagna*, but when her father deliberately insulted her husband it proved too much for her and she died. Shiva later wreaked havoc on Daksha's celebrations and took up the body of Sati on his shoulders and in a trance danced about the world, unmindful of his duties in the cycle of life. Then Lord Vishnu started cutting off portions of Sati's body, which fell in different parts of the world, from what is now Baluschistan to Assam. The fifty-one places where pieces of Sati's body fell all became shrines to the Shakti cult.

The Hindu temple or *mandir*, though generally built according to a fixed architectural plan, can vary in size from a small roadside structure no bigger than a room to a palatial building spread over acres of land. The structural plan of the temple is derived from that of Yagshala (hall of Vedic sacrifice).

Hindu gods and goddesses reside in the temple. The priests who act as the servants daily bathe, dress, garland and feed the deities. After the midday worship, the temple doors are shut so that the deities may rest.

The evening *puja*, alongwith the *aarti* ceremony is usually the most important event in the day's programme.

The heart of the Hindu temple is the inner sanctum, known as the *garbha-griha* (literally the womb). It houses the consecrated statue of the main deity and is the most sacred part of the temple. The consecration of the statue is an elaborate affair involving the recitation of sacred *mantras* and the performance of many complicated rituals. However once the rituals are complete the spirit of god is supposed to enter the statue and it becomes a symbol of the divine.

A *shikara* (a tapering tower or spire), often decorated with ornamental sculpture, is built above the inner sanctum. The stucture containing the *garbha-griha* is called the *vimana*. The devotees who visit the temple pay homage to the deities while standing in front of the *garbha-griha*. A large assembly area, often a hall with pillars, known as the *mandapa* is built in front of the *garbha-griha*. Steps called *antrata* connect the central hall to the main shrine. An *ardhmandapa*, a covered porch with steps coming down from the temple, is added to the *mandapa* wherever needed. Since circumabulating the deity is an essential part of the worship, many temples have a circular

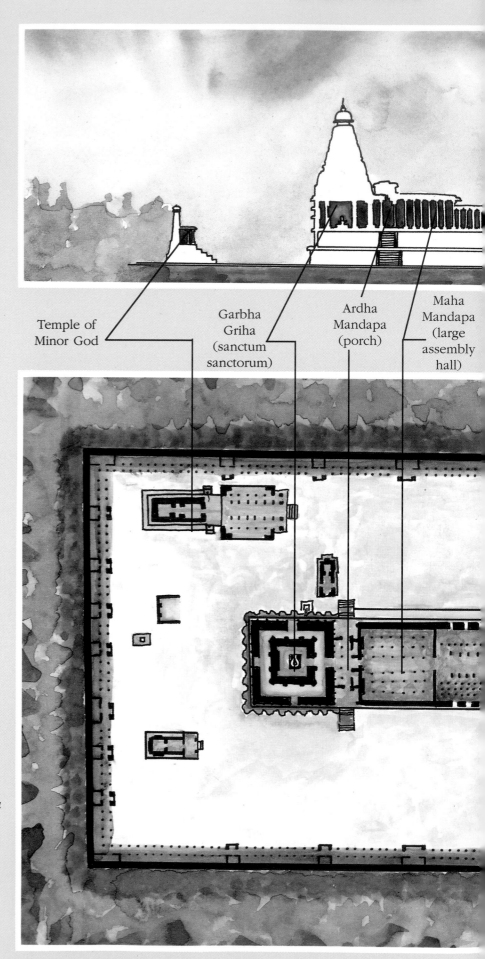

Temple of Minor God

Garbha Griha (sanctum sanctorum)

Ardha Mandapa (porch)

Maha Mandapa (large assembly hall)

Temple

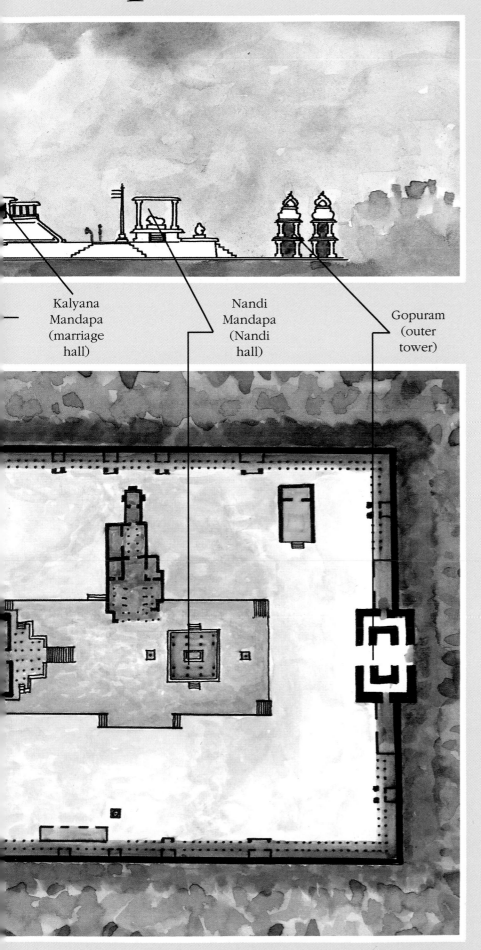

Kalyana Mandapa (marriage hall)

Nandi Mandapa (Nandi hall)

Gopuram (outer tower)

path around the inner sanctum called *pradakshina.*

Large temple complexes have a separate structure for preparation of food located at the northeast or southeast corner only. A shrine in front of the structure often houses the vehicle of the deity. This vehicle could be a bird or an animal which the deity rides, for example, the Garuda or eagle which is Vishnu's mount.

Apart from the main deity, a large temple often houses separate shrines for other associated deities—these could be structures for the consort of the main deity, or for deities like Hanuman or Ganesha, or places reserved for the chanting of *mantras.* They could be dancing halls for the temple dancers, or rooms for storing utensils.

A south Indian temple however, is different from the north Indian temple described above. In the south, the temple consists of three or four squares with the main shrine located in the innermost square.

The *parikrama,* or an open courtyard, is built between each square. Unlike a north Indian temple, the spire above the main shrine is often very short. The tallest structure in a temple in the south is the *gopuram,* which is a tower built in the centre of the outermost wall of the temple complex.

Gopurams are built on each of the four walls of the outer square. Those on the outermost walls are the tallest. A typical *gopuram* has a rectangular base but it tapers on all sides as it rises.

Subsidiary shrines dedicated to different deities are set against the boundary walls of the squares.

The elevation (above) and detailed plan (below) of a typical Hindu temple of south India.

The Ganga is regarded as the river of heaven that came down to earth to wash off the sins of suffering humanity. It is worshipped with lamps in traditional fashion during Kartik Purnima in October-November.

Chapter 6

CURRENT PRACTICES

When a Hindu goes to a temple he does not say he is going to worship. Instead he says he is going for a *darshan*. The term means seeing. In the spiritual sense it refers to a special kind of 'seeing' for the Hindu image is never an end in itself; rather, it is the means through which the vision is directed towards the ultimate divinity.

Darshan means being in the presence of the lord, beholding the divine image. Hindus take the trouble to go for *darshan* specially at those times of the day when the image is decked out in flowers and when offerings of water, food, incense, as well as camphor lamps are presented to the deity. After the *darshan*, the devotee receives *prasada*, the consecrated food offerings which carry the deity's blessings or grace.

Temple or domestic worship is known as *puja*. In the temple a trained staff of priests conducts the *puja*. The *puja* normally ends with the *aarti* (form of worship) after which the devotee performs *parikrama* (circumambulation).

Other acts of Hindu worship include *vrata* or ritual observances which a devotee undertakes for a fixed period of time stretching from a day to weeks or months, usually for a specific end. The *vrata* may include fasting, abstention and special observances; it usually includes the recitation of stories (*tatha*) which demonstrate the

effectiveness of the particular *vrata* which the devotee is undertaking. The term *tirtha* literally means 'fording' or 'crossing place'. For the Hindus, *tirthas* are sacred places so charged with religious merit and holy power that it is easy to cross over to the spiritual world from there. Going on pilgrimages and regularly visiting the *tirthas* is an important aspect of Hindu religious tradition and with all the modern-day improvements in communication, this is one traditional practice that has grown in strength over the years.

Most of the *tirthas* are associated with the great mythical acts of gods or epic heroes. Thus Kurukshetra is famous because the battle of the Mahabharata was said to have been fought there. Similarly the city of Ayodhya is associated with Rama and that of Mathura with Krishna. Stories associated with the *tirthas* are told in popular extolling literature called *mahatmyas*. These also list the immense benefits which accrue to the devotee who visits a holy place.

There are thousands of *tirthas* spread all over India, but a few have now gained in importance and are considered pre-eminent. These are the *saptpuris* or the seven cities: Ayodhya, Mathura, Haridwar, Varanasi, Kanchi, Dwarka and Ujjain. These destinations of pilgrimage are believed to bestow the ultimate gift of liberation on all those who die within their premises. Among all the *tirthas*, Kashi (Varanasi), is said to be the most important.

The *saptpuris* are followed by the four *dhams* (holiest of holies): Badrinath in the north (in the Himalayas), Puri in the east, Dwarka in the west, and Rameshwar in the south. Other sacred places include the 108 *pithas* (benches or seats) of Shakti, the divine female power, the twelve places where the Shiva *linga* is supposed to have burst forth on earth in a fiery column of light and the seven sacred rivers whose waters wash away the sins of a lifetime.

THE HINDU CALENDAR

For the Hindus, time is divided into three calendars—the lunar, the solar and the cosmic. The lunar calendar is used to determine the annual cycle of festivals, observances and other significant religious moments.

The lunar month faithfully follows the changing phases of the moon, and is divided into two 15-day *pakshas* or 'wings'. The first *paksha* of the month is the Krishna-paksha or the dark fortnight. This is the waning fortnight when the moon moves towards the new moon night *(amavasya)*. The second is the Shukla-paksha, or the bright fortnight, when the moon moves

The Kashi Vishvanath temple or the golden temple is the centre of Shiva worship for the whole of north India. It was plated with gold by Raja Ranjit Singh in 1839.

towards the full moon *(purnima)*. The lunar month is slightly shorter than the solar one, so every two or three years an extra month

Facing page: *The city of Madurai is* dvadasanta *(the subtle centre or* chakra *located in close proximity to the thousand-petalled lotus in the brain) where the goddess, Sri Minaksi, manifests herself in seven different forms: Bala, Bhuvaneshwari, Gauri, Matanga, Syama, Pancadasaksari, and Mahasodasi. Madurai is also famous for its* **rathyatra** *(car festival).*
Preceding pages 74-75: *The Ganga is sacred everywhere in India but it is especially sacred in the holy city of Varanasi. Thousands of worshippers gather daily on the riverfront and, half immersed in water, greet the rising sun. A ritual bath in the Ganga at Varanasi is said to wash away the sins of many a lifetime.*

is added to ensure that the lunar calendar matches the solar one and the festivals continue to be celebrated in their appropriate seasonal setting.

The Hindu solar calendar, like its Western counterpart, contains a cycle of seven 24-hour days within the larger 12-month yearly cycle. While the actual phase of the moon is used to describe the lunar day, like 'the fifth day of the waxing fortnight', each solar day is named after the deity which rules that particular day. Shani

Brahspati or Jupiter rules Brahspativara (Thursday); and Shukra or Venus rules Shukravara (Friday).

The twelve months of the calendar can be divided into 6 seasons, spring, summer, rainy season, autumn, winter, and the cool weather. The corresponding Hindu calendar is as follows:

1. *Vasanta* (Spring):
   Chaitra (March-April)
   Vaishakha (April-May)

Thousands of devotees vie with one another to draw the huge sixteen-wheeled chariot of Sri Jagannath (Lord of the Universe) to the Gundicha Temple in Puri. The event commemorates Lord Krishna's journey to Mathura from Gokula. Krishna killed the evil Kansa, king of Mathura during this legendary voyage.

or Saturn for example lends his name to Shanivara or Saturday. Ravi or the Sun is in charge of Ravivara (Sunday); Soma or the moon rules Somavara (Monday); Mangal or Mars rules Mangalvar (Tuesday); Buddha or Mercury rules Buddhavar (Wednesday);

Preceding pages 78-79: *Holi is a great springtime festival of gaiety and chaos. During the day, in homes and streets revellers splash or smear each others' faces with coloured water or powder. On this day social hierarchies and past animosities disappear. Everyone is equal and everyone is a friend. In the evening people exchange visits and offer sweets.*

2. *Grishma* (Summer):
   Jyaishtha (May-June)
   Ashadha (June-July)
3. *Varsha* (Rains):
   Shravan (July-August),
   Bhadrapada (August-September)
4. *Sharad* (Autumn):
   Ashwin, (September-October),
   Kartika (October-November)
5. *Hemanta* (Winter):
   Agrahanya, (November-December),
   Pausa (December -January)
6. *Shishira* (Cool season):
   Magha (January-February),
   Phalgun (February-March)

The Hindu new year begins with the bright fortnight of the spring month of Chaitra, and ends with the dark fortnight of Phalgun. The annual cycle of days and seasons merges with the cosmic cyclical time frame measured in terms of the *yugas*. Hindus believe that the world exists during the 'day' of Brahma and is dissolved and ceases to exist during the 'night' of Brahma. One day of Brahma however consists of four *yugas* multiplied a thousand times, each of which is measured in terms of the years of

For the devotees, the cosmic time frame grounded in mythology remains a living reality. The different time frames merge with one another. For example Lord Rama, the seventh incarnation of Vishnu, is said to have been born on the ninth day of the bright half of Chaitra in Ayodhaya (in north India) in the Treta Yuga. His birthday, Ram Navami, now a major Hindu festival, is celebrated on the ninth day of the bright half of Chaitra all over India.

The commencement of the four

The distinctive feature of the Kumbha Mela is that the ascetics of various sects who march down in a procession to the river are given bathing priority over common pilgrims. The various emblems displayed by the ascetics include the silver chattar *(canopy), sceptre, trumpet and the* gaddi *(seat of honour).*

the gods. Each great *yuga* is said to consist of 12,000 god-years. One human year is equal to a day and night of the gods, and hence one day of the gods is equal to 365 human years. The fantastic figures arrived at in using this system of calculation reassuringly keep the final dissolution of the world at a very distant date. However, Hindus insist that at the present moment we are living in the most degenerate of times—the Kali Yuga. The other three *yugas*—Satya, Treta, Dwapar—are all arranged in a descending hierarchy with the Krita Yuga thought of as the golden age, when true joy and righteousness prevailed.

mythical *yugas* or ages (Satya, Treta, Dvapara, and Kali) are also commemorated on the third day of the bright fortnight in Vaishakha, the ninth day of the bright fortnight in Kartika, the dark thirteenth day

*Following pages 82-83: It was at Vrindavan that Lord Krishna spent his childhood in the company of cowherds. The **Ras Lila** enacts scenes from Krishna's childhood.*
Following pages 84-85: Tonsuring is an act of purification, as the Hindus believe that impurities are entangled in the hair. Before their ritual dip during the Kumbha Mela devotees often get their heads shaved.

of Bhadra, and the full moon day in Magha respectively.

FESTIVALS

Holi: Holi is the vibrant springtime festival of colour celebrated all over India. The evening before the actual festivities start, a bonfire is lit and people sing and dance around it. Next day friends and relatives throw coloured water and coloured powder on each other. Exuberant processions of fantastically painted faces are taken out. In the evening, people put on their best clothes and visits are exchanged. The origin of the festival is shrouded in mystery, but in the popular mind it is invariably linked with the story of Prahlada, the great child devotee of Vishnu, whose father sought to have him killed by fire. By the grace of God, he escaped, but his evil aunt Holika, who was assigned the job of killing him, died. Holi symbolizes the triumph of good over evil.

Shiva Ratri: This is the most significant Shiva festival, and it is celebrated all over India. It marks the day when Shiva is said to have married Parvati, the daughter of the king of the Himalayas.

Pongal: The three-day Pongal festival is celebrated with special fervour in south India. The first day is known as Bhogi. The second day, known as Surya, is devoted to the worship of the sun, while the third day, Mattu, is devoted to the worship of cows and oxen.

Maker Sankranti: This is a north Indian festival celebrated simultaneously with Pongal in the south. The term 'sankranti' means the day when the sun passes from one zodiac sign to another. This day is considered to be particularly auspicious to bathe in the Ganga or any other holy waters. In Assam the festival is called Magha Bihu.

Rath Yatra: In Ashadha (June-July) the Rath Yatra, or the the chariot procession of Shri Jagannath is taken throughout the streets in a mighty procession. The festival is celebrated all over India but the main festival is held in Puri in Orissa.

Teej: Annually celebrated in Ashadha, the festival is sacred to Parvati, the consort of Lord Shiva. Women fast on this day and in some areas like Rajasthan processions bearing images of Parvati are taken out by devotees.

Guru Vyas Purnima: On full moon day in Ashadha, students pay their respects to their guru for on this festival day the teacher himself is the object of worship. It is also known as Vyas Purnima because Vyas, the author of the *Mahabharata*, is regarded as the archetype guru.

Ganga Dussehera: This festival is celebrated on the anniversary of the holy Ganga's descent on earth. A bath in the Ganga on this holy day is a must for the devout. Those who cannot reach the Ganga take a dip in any sacred stream nearby, thereby paying homage to the river of rivers. The river itself is worshipped and in many places thousands of lighted lamps are sent floating downstream.

Navratras: Literally the 'nine nights of the goddesses', this is a nine day festival devoted to the worship of goddesses. The Navratras fall twice in a year, once in spring and once in autumn. Of the two, the one in autumn called Durga Puja is more fervently celebrated. Beautifully made clay images of Durga are consecrated so that they become the dwelling place of the great goddess. On the tenth day these images are taken in a procession and committed to the river.

Raksha Bandhan: This festival honouring the brother-sister relationship is celebrated in the month of Shravan (July-August). On this day sisters tie an amulet-like thread called *rakhi* round the wrists of their brothers. The *rakhi* is an expression of the

*Facing page: During the Durga Puja festival (September-October) the emphasis is on the motherhood of God. Shakti, the female counterpart of the Impersonal Absolute is propitiated in the form of the Nava-(nine) Durgas. The fall **navratras** also occur now, during which the images of the nine Durgas are consecrated. On the tenth day—Vijaya Lakshmi, the day of victory of the Goddess over the bull-demon Mahisasura—the images are taken in procession to the river where the Goddess is given leave to depart and the images, now lifeless, are committed to the river.*

sister's best wishes and once tied, commits the brother to protect and help her.

Vasant Panchami: This festival marks the onset of spring and is celebrated on the fifth day of the bright half of Magha (January-February). The day is dedicated to Saraswati, the goddess of learning. Kama Deva, the the god of love (who bears a remarkable resemblance to Cupid), is also invoked on this day.

Dussehra: This 10-day festival in the month of Aswin (September-October) celebrates the great victory of Lord Rama over the demon king, Ravana. All over the country, Ram Lila—the dramatic enactment of scenes from the life of Rama—are performed. On the 10th day, known as Vijay Dashami, huge effigies of the ten-headed Ravana are set on fire, symbolizing the triumph of good over evil.

Diwali: At the end of the fortnight in the month of Kartika, on the new moon day Hindus celebrate Diwali—the festival of light. Every household is cleaned up and in the evening illuminated by rows of light. The goddess Lakshmi is honoured and worshipped. It is believed that on this night Lakshmi, the goddess of wealth and prosperity, roams the streets, visiting and bestowing blessings on houses that are neat and clean and well lit up. The merchant class specially honours the goddess on this day.

Ram Navami, the birthday of Lord Rama is a major Hindu festival celebrated in March-April. Also celebrated in the same month is **Hanuman Jayanti**, the birth anniversary of Hanuman. **Janmashthami**, the birthday of Lord Krishna and **Ganesha Chaturthi**, the birthday of Lord Ganesha, are both celebrated in the month of Bhadra (August-September).

In western India the Ganesha Chaturthi festival is celebrated with special fervour. Ganesha idols are taken out in procession before being immersed in the sea. Ganesha is the god of learning, wisdom and power, the presiding deity of Muldhara Chakra (plexus) or the psychic centre in the human body.
Following pages 90-91: *Diwali, one of the main festivals of India, celebrates the return of Rama to his rightful throne and symbolically the return of the good season.*

Hindu Sacraments

While the daily *puja* can be performed even at home, Hindu family rituals are more complicated and often entail the services of trained Brahmin priests. Those rituals and ceremonies that are called *samskaras* are the most important. These are very different from the Christian sacraments, though like the latter they too are instrumental in giving the Hindu a definite sense of identity within a social and religious framework.

The sacraments range from 16 to 40 in number. Different texts give different numbers of sacred ceremonies to be performed at different stages of life. Some of the most popular of these are discussed below.

Namakaran is the naming ceremony and is performed on the twelfth day after birth. It is both a religious and social occasion. Friends and relatives are invited to celebrate the birth of a child in the family.

Niskramana is performed when the child is taken out of the house for the first time. On that day, a square area in the open courtyard is marked with cowdung and the sign of the *swastika* is marked on it. Over it, grains of rice are scattered by the mother. The child is brought out and the ceremony ends when the father makes the child look at the sun while Vedic hymns are chanted in the background, accompanied by the auspicious blowing of the conch shell.

Annaprasana is performed when the child is fed for the first time, with sacramental food prepared to the chanting of Vedic *mantras*. Different preparations are prescribed for different impacts on the child. Oblations are offered to Vac (speech) and to Urja (vigour) as well as to other deities. Performed six months after the birth of the child, this rite ensures that the weaning of the child takes place at the proper time.

Mundan is a ceremony performed at the time of the first haircut of the baby, when all the hair is shaved off its head. This is meant to ensure a long life for the baby.

Karnvedhna is connected with the piercing of the ear of the baby between its first and fourth year. Apart from enabling the Hindu child, specially the girl child, to wear ornaments, the sacrament is meant to be good for the health of the baby.

Upanayana, the sacred thread ceremony, marks the initiation of the child into social life. It is entrusted to a teacher for education. The ceremony is usually performed between the age of 8 to 12 and is perhaps the most important childhood ceremony, specially among Brahmins.

Vivaha or marriage is easily the most central of the Hindu sacraments for it marks the initiation of the young male Hindu into the Gryhastha ashram. Till the time of marriage he is a student, but after marriage he becomes a householder responsible for all domestic rituals, sacrifices and ceremonies. The scriptures repeatedly assert that the entire edifice of Hindu religion rests on the shoulders of the householder. Most Hindu marriages are arranged marriages where the respective families bring the bride and the bridegroom together. The wedding ceremony nowadays lasts for a few hours, but traditionally it would carry on for four to five days. The rituals performed during a wedding vary greatly from region to region, caste to caste, but some of the more basic ones are: (a) the welcoming of the bridegroom and his party by the parents of the bride; (b) the giving away of the daughter by the parents; (c) making three wishes and tying

Facing page: Traditionally, a marriage was not a contractual but a sacred step in one's spiritual life. Marriage enabled a couple to enter the second (gryhastha) stage of life. The wife was considered ardhangini (the other half) of her husband and no religious ritual could be performed without her participation.

the symbolic marriage bond; (d) fastening
of the marriage necklace around the bride's
neck; (e) offerings for the sacred fire; (f)
the seven ritual steps; (g) the final
sprinkling of water on the couple by the
priests; and (h) the blessings given by the
parents and the assembled guests. These
rituals are accompanied by the chanting of
appropriate Vedic *mantras* and hymns.

Antyesthi or cremation is the last of
the Hindu sacraments and is designed to
ensure the good of the departed soul in
the next world. The term means 'the last
sacrifice'. The whole of the Hindu existence
is looked upon as a continuous sacrifice,
and death is celebrated as the last great
sacrificial act. Fire is regarded by the
Hindus as a messenger carrying offerings
from men to gods. During cremation, the
human body itself is offered as the last
sacrifice.

The dead body is carried on a specially
constructed wooden frame to the cremation
ground in a formal funeral procession. The
chief mourner, usually with a tonsured
head, is followed by relatives and friends
all chanting 'Ram Nam Satya Hai' (the name
of god is truth). At the cremation ground,
the body is washed and placed on a
specially prepared pyre made of dry wood.
Accompanied by the chanting of Vedic
mantras, the chief mourner lights the pyre.
On the eleventh day after the cremation an
offering of ten *pindas* (balls made up of
cooked rice) is made which is believed to
help the deceased acquire a new body for
the next existence. The annual *shraddha*
ceremony is observed by the living family
members in memory of the departed.

*It is said that at the dawn of creation Vishnu's
devotion to Lord Shiva so pleased the latter that
he shook with delight, causing his jewelled
(mani) earring (karnika) to fall into the
Chakrapushkarini kund. Shiva decreed that the
spot where his earring fell be named Manikarnika. The spot became the world's first pool
and first* tirtha, *dug out and filled by Vishnu
himself. The cremation ground immediately to
its south is called Manikarnika, though its
sanctity is due to its being in Banaras.*

FURTHER READINGS

1. Basham, A. L. *The Origins and Development of Classical Hinduism.* Delhi. Oxford University Press, 1990.
2. Biardeau, Madeleine. *Hinduism: The Anthropology of a Civilization.* Delhi. Oxford University Press, 1989.
3. Chakravarthy, Sitansu S. *Hinduism: A Way of Life.* Delhi. Motilal Banarsi Das, 1991.
4. Coomaraswamy, Ananda K. *The Dance of Shiva.* New Delhi. Munshiram Manoharlal, 1982.
5. Dange, S. S. *Hindu Domestic Rituals: A Critical Glance.* Delhi. Ajanta Publications, 1985.
6. Dowson, John. *A Classical Dictionary of Hindu Mythology and Religion.* New Delhi. Heritage Publisher, 1992.
7. Eck, Diana. *Banaras: City of Light.* London. Routledge & Kegan Paul, 1983.
8. O'Flaherty W. D. *Siva: The Erotic Ascetic.* London. Oxford University Press, 1973.
9. Pereira, Jose. *Hindu Theology.* Delhi. Motilal Banarasi Das, 1976.
10. Sinha, B. C. *Hinduism and Symbol Worship.* Delhi. Agam Kala Prakashan, 1983.
11. Butenein, Van. *The Mahabharata* (translator and editor). Chicago. University of Chicago Press, 1973.
12. Wilkins, W. J *Hindu Mythology.* Delhi. Rupa and Co., 1994. First Edition, 1982.